Charles King

Ending Civil Wars

Adelphi Paper 308

Oxford University Press, Great Clarendon Street, Oxford OX2 6DP
Oxford New York
Athens Auckland Bangkok Bombay Calcutta Cape Town
Dar es Salaam Delhi Florence Hong Kong Istanbul Karachi
Kuala Lumpur Madras Madrid Melbourne Mexico City
Nairobi Paris Singapore Taipei Tokyo Toronto
and associated companies in
Berlin Ibadan

Oxford is a trade mark of Oxford University Press

Published in the United States
by Oxford University Press Inc., New York

© The International Institute for Strategic Studies 1997

First published March 1997 by **Oxford University Press** for
The International Institute for Strategic Studies
23 Tavistock Street, London WC2E 7NQ

Director Dr John Chipman
Deputy Director Rose Gottemoeller
Editor Dr Gerald Segal
Assistant Editor Cathy Brannon
Production Supervisor Mark Taylor

British Library Cataloguing in Publication Data
Data available

Library of Congress Cataloguing in Publication Data

ISBN 0-19-829343-7
ISSN 0567-932x

contents

illustrations

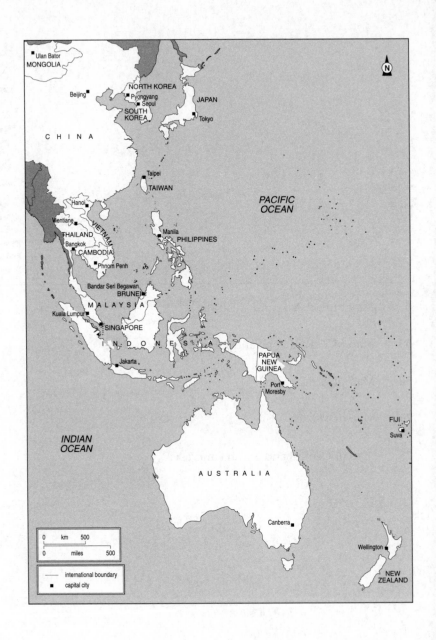

glossary

FRELIMO .... *Frente para a Libertação de Moçambique*

FSLN .... *Frente Sandinista de Liberación Nacional (Nicaragua)*

G .... Incumbent government

GIA .... *Groupe Islamique Armée* (Algeria)

IFOR .... Implementation Force (Bosnia)

IFP .... Inkatha Freedom Party (South Africa)

IMT .... Islamic Movement of Tajikistan

INA .... Iraqi National Accord

INC .... Iraqi National Congress

IRA .... Irish Republican Army (United Kingdom)

KDP .... Kurdistan Democratic Party (Iraq)

KNU .... Karen National Union (Myanmar)

LAK .... Liberation Army of Kosovo (Federal Republic of Yugoslavia)

LRA .... Lord's Resistance Army (Uganda)

LTTE .... Liberation Tigers of Tamil Eelam (Sri Lanka)

MILF .... Moro Islamic Liberation Front (Philippines)

MINUGUA .... United Nations Human Rights Verification Mission in Guatemala

MINURSO .... United Nations Mission for the Referendum in Western Sahara

MNLF .... Moro National Liberation Front (Philippines)

MPLA .... *Movimento Popular para a Libertação de Angola*

MQM .... Mohajir National Movement (Pakistan)

MRTA .... *Movimiento Revolucionario Túpac Amaru* (Peru)

NCGUB .... National Coalition Government of the Union of Burma

NDA .... National Democratic Alliance (Sudan)

NGO .... Non-governmental organisation

NPA .... New People's Army (Philippines)

NSCN .... National Socialist Council of Nagaland (India)

ONUMOZ	United Nations Operation in Mozambique
ONUSAL	United Nations Observer Mission in El Salvador
OSCE	Organisation for Security and Cooperation in Europe
PKK	Kurdistan Workers' Party (Turkey)
PLAM	People's Liberation Army of Manipur (India)
POLISARIO	*Frente Popular para la Liberación de Saguia el-Hamra y de Río de Oro* (Western Sahara)
PUK	Patriotic Union of Kurdistan (Iraq)
RENAMO	*Resistência Nacional Moçambicana*
RUF	Revolutionary United Front (Sierra Leone)
SCIRI	Supreme Council of the Islamic Revolution in Iraq
SFOR	Stabilisation Force (Bosnia)
SLA	South Lebanon Army
SPLA	Sudanese People's Liberation Army (Sudan)
ULIMO-J	United Liberation Movement – Roosevelt Johnson faction (Liberia)
UNAVEM I, II and III	United Nations Angola Verification Mission
UNDOF	United Nations Disengagement Observer Force (Syria/Israel)
UNFICYP	United Nations Peacekeeping Force in Cyprus
UNGOMAP	United Nations Good Offices Mission in Afghanistan and Pakistan
UNIFIL	United Nations Interim Force in Lebanon
UNITA	*União Nacional para a Independência Total de Angola*
UNMIBH	United Nations Mission in Bosnia and Herzegovina
UNMOP	United Nations Mission of Observers in Prevlaka
UNMOT	United Nations Mission of Observers in Tajikistan

UNOMIG .... United Nations Observer Mission in Georgia

UNOMIL .... United Nations Observer Mission in Liberia

UNOSOM I and II .... United Nations Operation in Somalia

UNPROFOR .... United Nations Protection Force (Bosnia)

UNSMA .... United Nations Special Mission in Afghanistan

UNTAC .... United Nations Transitional Authority in Cambodia

UNTAES .... United Nations Transitional Administration for Eastern Slavonia, Baranja and Western Sirmium (Croatia)

UNTSO .... United Nations Truce Supervision Organisation (Israel)

URNG .... *Unidad Revolucionaria Nacional Guatemalteca*

Thinking about how wars end has long been a major task of policy-makers and statesmen. Whether to declare victory, sue for peace or begin negotiations with the enemy were questions raised on all sides during the First and Second World Wars, and in Korea, Vietnam, Afghanistan and scores of other international disputes. Today, however, instead of deciding when to end a war they started, world powers are most often confronted with the issue of how to stop wars in which they are not involved as belligerents and in which their own immediate strategic interests are unclear. Most contemporary wars, moreover, have involved armed conflict within states rather than between them. United Nations peacekeeping operations in Cambodia, Somalia, former Yugoslavia and elsewhere, the NATO-led peace Implementation Force (IFOR) and Stabilisation Force (SFOR) in Bosnia, and Russian and Commonwealth of Independent States (CIS) deployments in Georgia, Tajikistan and Moldova have all been designed to separate warring parties, provide secure environments for carrying out humanitarian relief projects, facilitate negotiations among belligerents or aid political and economic reconstruction after a peace settlement has been signed. The fighting itself, not any particular belligerent party, is typically seen as the interveners' main adversary.

Much of the contemporary debate about external involvement in civil wars centres around two issues: first, how to define 'success' in such operations and second, how to relate the short-term task of halting the fighting to the longer-term projects of ensuring a stable peace and promoting post-war reconstruction. In both instances, however, external involvement is sometimes judged less in terms of its impact on the termination of the conflict and more in terms of its effects on the intervening state or coalition of states. If an operation can be completed on time, with minimal loss of blood and treasure and with relations between the various members of the intervening coalition in relatively good repair, it is normally seen as successful. Interventions can thus become narcissistic, with questions about the long-term effects of external involvement pushed to the back of the queue. There are many studies about intervention in civil wars – either military or otherwise – but very little on the relationship

interventions can become narcissistic

between external intervention and the outcome of the conflicts themselves, or on why some efforts at mediation fail and others succeed.[1] Why do belligerents in civil wars decide to stop fighting? What obstacles exist to concluding and implementing negotiated settlements? How might third parties contribute to a stable and durable peace accord? These are all questions often overlooked in discussions about the efficacy of intervention.

Knowing more about the internal dynamics of sub-state military contests is an important part of assessing the relationship between intervention and durable peace, and an important corrective to contemporary discussions about the role of external powers in such disputes. But as this paper will argue, thinking about civil wars and how they end presents policy-makers with a serious dilemma. On the one hand, most civil wars have ended with the outright military victory of one side over the other, and the most stable peace settlements have been achieved more readily through military victory than through negotiations. On the other hand, military victory in civil wars is also often associated with widespread human-rights abuses, atrocities, genocide, environmental degradation and a host of other ills which make economic reconstruction and political reconciliation especially difficult. Judging by the historical evidence, then, the choice for external powers seems to be between allowing civil wars to 'run their course' and risk massive levels of human suffering and physical destruction, or to promote a negotiated settlement which, if it can ever be reached, may be inherently unstable.

There are various explanations for this dilemma. Some observers attribute the protracted and often vicious nature of civil wars to the belligerents' irrational motives. Ancient hatreds, religious fervour or loyalty to kith and kin are said to explain why some civil wars drag on even past the stage when it would seem to be in the best interest of belligerents to cease. There are also those who argue that the incompatible identities and values at the base of violent conflicts make compromise extremely difficult. Belligerents are so committed to the ends for which they originally took up arms – defence of a homeland, creation of an ethnically pure state, dominance of political institutions by their own communal group – that the space for negotiations is necessarily limited. In this view, parties to the conflict are not necessarily irrational; it may, in fact, be quite reasonable for the parties to advocate creating an independent homeland in the face of oppression by a rival communal group. Nevertheless, the strongly held beliefs, identities and cultural values that divide belligerents can preclude their reaching a compromise settlement at the negotiating table.

All civil wars clearly contain some elements of these factors. There are, however, additional explanations for the difficulty belligerents often face in both reaching and implementing negotiated settlements. These concern what might be called the 'structural' elements of war-fighting in internal conflicts, that is, the array of incentives to continue the violence and the disincentives for compromise which arise during the course of the conflict itself and which can inhibit the willingness of the contesting sides both to engage in negotiations and to abide by the terms of peace settlements.

This paper argues that understanding these structural components – discussed in detail in Chapter 2 – can contribute to the development of more realistic strategies for dealing with civil wars. External agents are unlikely to have a great deal of influence over the elements of irrationality and contested values and identities that underlie many protracted conflicts. But at the margins, intervening powers can affect the structure of incentives for continued violence and influence the calculations of belligerents about the benefits of negotiated settlement. After the fighting has stopped, external powers can also help former belligerents build a stable peace by augmenting the motives which prompted the descent into warfare in the first place. Of course, there is no single template that can be applied to all civil wars. The origins and evolution of internal conflicts, like the decisions of external powers to intervene, are to a great degree idiosyncratic. But in cases in which external actors – whether individual states or multilateral organisations – perceive that 'doing something' about a particular internal conflict is in their own interest, understanding the system of incentives for violence from the perspective of the belligerents themselves is an important starting point in crafting a pragmatic and effective strategy of involvement.

chapter 1

How Civil Wars End: Problems and Patterns

Everything in war is simple, Clausewitz wrote, but the simplest thing is very difficult. This dictum is especially apposite in the case of wars that take place within the boundaries of internationally recognised states. The reasons for which civil wars are fought, the levels of organisation among the various contesting parties, the degree of involvement by external powers and the political outcomes of such contests have all varied widely. This chapter begins with an overview of the complexity of civil wars and the difficulties inherent in generalisation about their origins and outcomes. Subsequent sections assess the record of negotiated settlements in civil wars and their durability, and explore common explanations for why protracted conflicts usually end in the military victory of one of the belligerent parties.

The Complexity of Intra-state Warfare

Since the Second World War, there have been at least 90 armed conflicts that might be classed as 'civil wars', ranging from the struggle between the Greek government and communist insurgents in the late 1940s through the myriad protracted conflicts in Latin America, Africa and East Asia from the 1950s, to the wars of the Yugoslav and Soviet successions in the 1990s.[1] In 1995, all the world's majors wars were fought within states rather than between them; by the middle of 1996, around two dozen 'hot' civil wars were in progress, while many others had been temporarily halted by the

signing of cease-fires and interim agreements.[2] Central authorities in
Algeria faced serious threats from the well-organised *Front Islamique
du Salut* (FIS) and the *Groupe Islamique Armée* (GIA). Struggles in
Afghanistan between a plethora of religious, ethnic and clan-based
factions, some of them supported by Iran and Pakistan, continued
unabated. In Indonesia, the issue of potential successors to President
Suharto raised questions about the likelihood of renewed large-scale
violence in East Timor and Irian Jaya; the spillover of the latter to
Papua New Guinea would further threaten a government already
beset by low-level separatist violence on its eastern-most island,
Bougainville. Restive Kurdish and Tamil minorities in Turkey and
Sri Lanka continued their bids for autonomy, as did the remnants of
the once-powerful Karen National Union (KNU) in Myanmar.
Fighting persisted among separatist ethnic groups in the Russian
Federation, while an uneasy truce was in place in Azerbaijan.
Central authority in Sudan and Somalia had effectively collapsed as
a result of internal armed conflicts, the spectre of communal violence
swept over relatively stable states such as Kenya and a host of other
African countries were plagued by simmering communal and
political disputes. Despite the successful termination of civil wars in
Nicaragua and El Salvador, high levels of organised political
violence continued in Colombia and Peru. Although lower in
intensity, Mexico's battles with the *Ejército Zapatista de Liberación
Nacional* (EZLN) proved to be a major threat to a government already
beset by allegations of corruption and links with drug traffickers.

A 1996 report by a US inter-agency task force estimated the
total number of persons directly threatened by such conflicts to be
around 42 million; in 1994, total foreign aid to victims of internal
wars reached an annual high of $7.2 billion.[3] The cost of these
conflicts in terms of casualties, destruction of property, lost trade and
investment, refugees and environmental degradation is impossible
to gauge. In civil wars, non-combatants are often seen as legitimate
targets by warring parties, and distinguishing between battle-related
deaths and politically motivated massacres is a futile exercise.
Drought, famine and disease also take their toll on soldiers and
civilians alike, and such 'natural' disasters can themselves become
skilfully wielded instruments of warfare. Even after the fighting
stops, anti-personnel mines and other unexploded ordnance wreak

havoc on civilian populations, and the wartime bonds forged among soldiers often form the basis for criminal networks in peacetime. In Angola, Afghanistan, Sierra Leone and elsewhere, the distinctions between war and peace, legality and lawlessness, security and disorder are normally lost on the war-zone's inhabitants. Even the lines between warring parties can sometimes fade away, with government and rebel forces actually working together to exploit non-combatant populations. Such cooperation can prolong the conflict rather than shorten it, as local élites amicably divide the spoils of war with their erstwhile enemies. As one observer has remarked, some civil wars can thus become very civil indeed.[4]

In addition, no civil war today is ever wholly internal. Because of concern over widespread human-rights abuses, the threat that warfare will spread to neighbouring states and the international economic effects of large-scale internal violence, international actors have taken a serious interest in the evolution and outcome of ongoing and latent conflicts. Since 1991, Russia has intervened directly to halt domestic disputes in Georgia, Moldova and Tajikistan. France has initiated unilateral military interventions in several African crises in recent years, such as *Opération Almandin* (May 1996) which foiled a rebellion by disaffected soldiers in the Central African Republic. The Organisation for Security and Cooperation in Europe (OSCE) has been particularly active in establishing permanent missions and facilitating negotiations in the conflict zones of the former Soviet Union. The United States continues to label narco-terrorism a major national-security threat and has pressured the governments of Colombia and Peru

no civil war today is ever wholly internal

to combat coalitions of drug traffickers and leftist guerrillas, going so far as to revoke the visa of Ernesto Samper, the Colombian head of state in July 1996. Most spectacularly, since early 1989, the UN has launched more than 20 major observer and peacekeeping missions, with the vast majority devoted to quelling internal conflicts and reducing the suffering of non-combatant populations. These include monitoring the withdrawal of foreign troops, supervising elections and demobilising combatants in Angola (UNAVEM I, II and III);

policing cease-fire agreements in Liberia (UNOMIL), Georgia (UNOMIG) and Western Sahara (MINURSO); implementing peace accords in El Salvador (ONUSAL), Cambodia (UNTAC) and Mozambique (ONUMOZ); and delivering humanitarian relief in Bosnia (UNPROFOR) and Somalia (UNOSOM I and II). Although the size and number of UN operations have been scaled back since their zenith in 1993, by late 1995 there were still some 59,000 troops deployed under UN auspices in 16 countries, with UN member-states contributing various numbers of personnel ranging from 7,500 soldiers from France to one from Albania.[5]

Understanding the Dynamics of Civil War

This active intervention in internal conflicts has been matched by a growing interest among policy analysts and academics in the nature of intra-state warfare and the ways in which civil wars end. Building on a much older tradition of strategic thought about war endgames in conflicts between states, researchers have extended their work to cover the topic of how violent conflicts among sub-state actors come to a close. How do wars waged within the boundaries of a recognised state differ from those between states? What accounts for the brutal and vicious nature of many internal conflicts? What causes belligerents in civil wars to lay down their arms? Each of these questions has been addressed in a growing body of analytical work on the dynamics of internal wars and their termination.

Problems of Definition and Prediction

So far there has been little agreement on the main issues at stake in the study of civil wars and how they end. In the first place, even determining what counts as a 'civil war' is more a matter of political perceptions than objective realities. Contemporary historians have already termed the entire 1914–45 period the age of Europe's 'great civil war'. Chroniclers of the next century may well see the myriad armed struggles in Chechnya, Bosnia, Tajikistan and elsewhere as part of one great 'war of the Communist succession'. A surfeit of terms has been used to describe large-scale organised violence within states – insurgencies, coups, revolutions, terrorism, small wars, limited wars, internal conflicts, low-intensity conflicts – but no obvious criteria have been set for distinguishing among them.

How one labels an armed conflict, in fact, normally has little to do with the nature of the conflict itself. In the 1970s, the *Financial Times* used the phrase 'small wars' as a catch-all term for stories about any internal conflict that might be used to fill space on the foreign pages.[6] Likewise, US military doctrine, which in recent years has accorded greater attention to sub-state military conflict, is remarkably abstruse on how to define it, using criteria as diverse as the character of the belligerents, their goals, their methods or the level of deadly force needed to frustrate any of the above.[7] The label bestowed on an internal conflict is also frequently determined by the political stance of the observer. Describing an armed conflict as a 'rebellion' or an 'insurgency' removes any legitimacy from the political aspirations of one of the contesting sides and

what counts as a civil war is often in the eye of the beholder

buttresses the claims of the incumbent government. On the other hand, employing the term 'civil war' indicates that all sides to the conflict have rational political goals which they are attempting to realise through the use of military force. What counts as a civil war is thus often in the eye of the beholder.[8]

Stating precisely when a civil war – however the term is defined – has ended is also a perplexing enterprise. As Quincy Wright wrote, the word 'permanent' in peace treaties, if it has any meaning at all, usually covers at most 20 years.[9] Thirty years of peace in Lebanon and Colombia, after civil wars in both countries in the 1940s and 1950s, may be as close to permanence as is possible in some societies.[10] In the Colombian case, the widespread violence that began in the late 1940s decreased significantly with the conclusion of a power-sharing arrangement between the rival Liberal and Conservative parties in 1958. But the social distrust spawned by the period of *la violencia* and the exclusion of leftist factions from the power-sharing framework ultimately ensured the resumption of large-scale violence in the late 1970s. Likewise, in Angola, international mediators hailed the brokering of the Bicesse accords in May 1991 as the final step in ending the 16-year conflict between the government and forces of the *União Nacional para a Independência Total de Angola* (UNITA). But UNITA leader Jonas Savimbi's refusal to accept the outcome of the September 1992 presidential elections, in which he lost in the first round to Eduardo dos Santos, once again plunged the country into war. At several points in Sri Lanka's war against Tamil separatists peace has seemed imminent, from the signing of an accord between New Delhi and Colombo in July 1987 to the government's massive *Operation Riviresa* against the Liberation Tigers of Tamil Eelam (LTTE) in late 1995 and 1996. But in each case, serious fighting flared again between Tamil and government forces. The signing of the Paris Agreement in October 1991 paved the way for the UN's comprehensive peace implementation mission in Cambodia, but by June 1992 the Khmer Rouge had to some extent undermined the settlement by rejecting the complete demobilisation of its fighting forces. Even the US Civil War, which formally ended with General Robert E. Lee's surrender in 1865, continued for years as a guerrilla struggle in which the level of violence in some southern states probably equalled that of modern low-intensity internal conflicts.[11]

A similar problem exists with attempts to define the most important catalysts for intra-state violence and to predict where civil wars are most likely to occur. As Donald Horowitz has noted, any reasonable analyst looking at Malaysia (Malaya) and Sri Lanka (Ceylon) at the time of their independence from British rule would have concluded that the likelihood of civil war in the former was far higher than in the latter. In Malaya, ethnic Malays represented only a slim majority against large Chinese and Indian minorities. These minorities were relatively recent arrivals and were viewed by the majority population as unwelcome guests. Ethnic relations in the country had been strained by an anti-Japanese and, later, anti-British and anti-Malay insurgency led by ethnic Chinese. There was no tradition of inter-communal accommodation. In the colonial period, ethnic élites were educated

there has been little agreement on when conflict has come to a definitive end

and trained in separate systems, and Malay politicians rarely sought to gain votes outside their narrow ethnic constituencies. In Ceylon, by contrast, the Tamil minority accounted for only about one-tenth of the total population. With the exception of a small community of immigrants from southern India, most Tamils had lived on the island for centuries and were considered by the majority Sinhalese as a constituent component of the Ceylonese nation. Tamil and Sinhalese élites mixed freely in the same schools and universities, and inter-communal bargaining was an ordinary part of political life. But by the mid-1990s, Sri Lanka was embroiled in a bloody and protracted civil war over the fate of Tamil areas on the north and east of the island. Malaysia, on the other hand, had experienced no serious out-break of violence since the summer of 1969.[12]

Because of these difficulties, it is impossible to point to any objective and universal criteria for what constitutes a civil war and what factors are likely, in all cases, to hasten its end. Despite the many books and articles on 'conflict resolution' and a growing body of work on 'war termination' in both inter- and intra-state conflicts, there has been little agreement on precisely what either of these phrases means or on how to determine when a large-scale armed conflict – whether within or between states – has come to a definitive end. It is illustrative of the lack of clarity on this issue, in fact, that the most frequently cited work in the war-termination field, Fred Iklé's classic *Every War Must End*, never defines either what constitutes a war or what defines its endpoint.[13] The concept of 'war termination', for example, has been described as:

- the process by which belligerents agree on the cessation of hostilities, a formal cease-fire or a peace agreement;
- the acceptance by all sides of the military outcome as the basis for determining the political outcome of a conflict;
- the process by which élites on all sides secure the agreement of their colleagues to press for peace; and
- the stage at which élites decide that the expected utility of continuing to fight is less than that of a settlement.[14]

The same can be said of the much larger field of 'conflict resolution', a term that has now filtered from psychology and industrial relations into the lexicon of international affairs and security studies.[15]

The number of variables used to explain how wars end is even larger, including the role of key leaders, the relative power balance among belligerents, the machinations of bureaucrats and military planners and the number of battle casualties suffered by each side. In terms of their general approach to the subject, analysts and scholars have taken equally diverse paths. Some have focused on the normative imperative to end all forms of violence, others have examined the economic incentives for beginning and ending wars and still others have seen war termination in terms of international law. Several have viewed war termination as a problem for diplomatic historians, while some have employed a range of contemporary theories of international relations to explain why and when wars come to a close.[16]

Because of the definition problems outlined above, making generalisations about internal armed conflicts is extremely perilous. The causes and evolution of civil wars are always to a large extent idiosyncratic, and the levels of foreign interest and involvement in bringing them to an end vary widely. Determining what counts as a 'civil war' and when it can reasonably be said to have ended also depends on rather arbitrary criteria, and those criteria in turn depend on the differing perceptions of belligerents, the interests of external powers, and the conventions of analysts and academics engaged in the study of warfare. The old bromide that one person's terrorist is another person's freedom fighter is as applicable to conceptual treatments of war-making as to the perceptions of international policy-makers, although for rather different reasons.

A cursory overview of the shape of recent war endings illustrates the inherent difficulties of generalisation. The ways in which these civil wars have moved towards a conclusion have been so varied that determining either the necessary or sufficient conditions for war termination seems nearly impossible. Cease-fires were a crucial first step towards negotiations in Cambodia, but in Angola, El Salvador and Nicaragua talks on ending the war began long before cease-fires were agreed. A constitutional formula for power-sharing was critical to ending the violence in South Africa, but such a framework was rejected in El Salvador, Mozambique, Namibia, Nicaragua and Zimbabwe.[17] In Sri Lanka, Moldova and Liberia, peacekeeping forces were deployed without the consent of all parties to the conflict; the absence of one insurgent group from the settlement talks undermined the credibility of the agreements in Sri Lanka and Liberia, but such a formula was crucial to building peace in Moldova. The case of Guatemala has been perhaps the most unusual in terms of the sequence of events on the road to peace. After signing a framework peace agreement in 1991, the Guatemalan government and the *Unidad Revolucionaria Nacional Guatemalteca* (URNG) were unable to agree on a

making generalisations about internal armed conflicts is extremely perilous

comprehensive cease-fire until December 1996. However, in the intervening period, they signed and began to implement accords on human-rights guarantees (March 1994), the investigation of past human-rights violations (June 1994), resettlement of displaced persons (June 1994), the rights of indigenous peoples (March 1995) and agrarian reform (May 1996).

Conflict, Negotiations and Political Stability

The complexity of large-scale organised violence within states thus makes specific predictions about outcomes impossible. At the most abstract level, however, four broad patterns are evident. First, the levels of violence in civil wars and the viciousness with which they are prosecuted are particularly high. As many as 1.2 million people may have been killed in Afghanistan since the outbreak of civil war in 1978, with another 5.2m possibly displaced. In Sudan, fighting between the government and the two main factions of the Sudanese People's Liberation Army (SPLA) has claimed an estimated 1.2m lives since the early 1980s, with another 4.5m fleeing conflict areas as refugees. Since 1992, renewed fighting between the Angolan government and UNITA has increased the country's total casualty figures since independence to around 800,000 and has prompted the flight of as many as 4m refugees.[18] As a result of the conflicts in former Yugoslavia, by 1996 some 700,000 refugees were living in other parts of Europe and 690,000 in the Yugoslav successor states, with another

1.3m persons internally displaced within Bosnia.[19] Between 1980 and 1992, the Peruvian Army's fight against *Sendero Luminoso* guerrillas drove as many as 600,000 peasants from their homes in the central Andean highlands and the Amazon basin, and led to the growth of sprawling, impoverished shanty towns (*pueblos jóvenes*) on the outskirts of Lima.[20] There is, of course, no objective measure of the magnitude of violence in civil wars as compared with other forms of sub-state violence, for levels of conflict wax and wane in the course of any single dispute. The level of public tolerance for organised violence also differs from society to society; violence that might be considered seriously destabilising in some countries has become a way of life in others. In most civil wars, however, the intensity of violence and the derivative grievances which it can produce present particular problems to those interested in ending the conflict via negotiations.

a negotiated peace has been a relatively rare outcome

Second, large-scale violence within states tends to be protracted, much more so than wars between states. Once opposing groups turn to violence as a way of settling their differences, the chances of a quick end have normally been remote. According to one calculation, inter-state wars in this century have lasted on average around 20 months, whereas civil wars have normally dragged on for 120 months or more.[21]

Third, despite the international community's interest in promoting the settlement of sub-state conflicts at the bargaining table, negotiated peace has been a relatively rare outcome. According to Paul Pillar, whereas over two-thirds of all inter-state wars waged since 1800 have ended via negotiation, only about one-third of civil wars have been settled in a similar manner.[22] For the post-Second World War period, Roy Licklider found that only about a quarter of civil wars have ended via negotiations.[23] When colonial wars and other conflicts with a substantial international component are eliminated, Stephen Stedman found that the figure for negotiated settlements stood at only 15%.[24] In the case of 'ethnic civil wars', internal conflicts in which the main belligerents are drawn from distinct communal groups, Chaim Kaufmann concluded that only 8 of 27 such conflicts since 1944 have ended in a negotiated settlement that did not lead to the partition of the state.[25] Although the exact figures on civil war endings differ (depending on how individual conflicts are coded), the common conclusion seems clear. While external powers today work assiduously to encourage belligerents to settle their differences at the negotiating table rather than on the battlefield, such attempts run against the tide of history.

Fourth, when belligerents have been able to sign a peace accord, either on their own or with the assistance of outside mediators, negotiations have historically produced more unstable settlements than those resulting from the outright victory of one side. Using separate lists of conflicts, Roy Licklider and Barbara Walter found that negotiated settlements have led to renewed warfare within five years in about 50% of cases.[26] The suggestion here is that, as in other areas of political life, justice and stability in war endings can often be at odds. While a negotiated settlement might produce a more equitable outcome than victory by one side, it also seems likely to foster renewed violence in the short to medium term.

Obstacles to Settlement: Three Views

Three explanations for these general characteristics can be found. In one view, the protracted and often vicious nature of sub-state violence, the inability of parties to engage in negotiations and the fragility of peace settlements themselves can be attributed mainly to the powerful emotions of belligerents.[27] War is an emotional enterprise, and the drive to redress past wrongs by perpetrating even more heinous crimes in the present can be so overwhelming that belligerents find themselves unable to contemplate any form of compromise with their opponents. The fervour of religious belief or the mystical ties of blood and land can plunge otherwise peaceful communities into violent conflict. In some instances, violence itself may be glorified, with the perverse thrill of death and destruction overshadowing the combatants' rational interest in stopping the fighting. According to this view, the goals for which belligerents enter into an armed conflict, their motives for continuing the struggle and their assessments of the costs they are willing to bear in pursuit of their objectives are less a matter of rational calculation and more a question of blind sentiment. Civil wars are thus analogous to epidemics: once violence erupts, it is likely to follow its own course, quite apart from the needs and desires of those caught up in the struggle; outside powers may seek to contain the conflict or inoculate neighbouring peoples against infection, but an end to the fighting will not be reached until the violence has effectively run its course.[28]

In a new edition of its famous report on the 1912–13 Balkan wars, the Carnegie Commission drew an explicit parallel between the atrocities of Bulgarian, Turkish and Serbian troops in the early part of this century and the crimes committed during the Yugoslav wars of the 1990s. Western policy-makers, warned George Kennan in his introduction to the new edition, would do well to consider those 'deeper traits of character inherited ... from a distant tribal past' which stood at the base of the conflict and which would inevitably frustrate 'the ability of the Balkan peoples to interact peaceably with one another'.[29] This view has also in recent years had a powerful impact on the shape of Western policy. If Washington pundits are to be believed, President Bill Clinton's reading of *Balkan Ghosts*, a journalistic sketch of the power of ethnic allegiances in the Balkans, may in part account for the us administration's early inability to decide in what measure Bosnia represented an ethnically motivated civil war or a case of international aggression, and its concomitant vacillation over an appropriate policy response.[30] Such wars, then, have little hope of ending in anything short of a decisive military victory by one side. Wars of this kind only end when somebody wins.[31]

understanding the structure of violence can uncover avenues of influence

A second, and more widely held, view holds that the real difficulty with promoting negotiated settlements and their implementation lies in the incompatible values and identities that belligerents bring to the conflict and that become hardened by the experience of war itself. Negotiated settlements have been rare precisely because the main prerequisite for negotiations – a willingness to compromise on the shape of the final peace settlement – is not often found in conflicts over strongly held beliefs and identities.[32] In this view, there is nothing inherently irrational about ethnic attachment, communal allegiance or religious solidarity; in fact, values and identities may to some extent reflect other social boundaries such as economic class. However, the strength of these social ties is often so great that, short of outright partition, negotiated settlements are unlikely, hence Kaufman's finding that communal conflicts settled via negotiation usually involve the territorial partition of the state. In addition, if the settlement fails to take into account the contested values and identities of the belligerents themselves – as well as the ways both may have become more entrenched as a result of the war – they can return to haunt peace settlements even after the 'successful' conclusion of a negotiated agreement.

Clearly, both views are to some extent correct. Individual combatants in civil wars frequently commit atrocities with a zeal that seems nothing short of irrational. Likewise, the deeply rooted cultural values and communal identities of belligerents sometimes preclude compromise on such basic issues as the territorial configuration of the state or the dominance of particular groups in the structures of government. There is, however, yet a third set of factors which helps account for the intractability of civil wars and the relative scarcity of durable negotiated settlements. This concerns what might be called the 'structure' of conflict itself: the system of incentives for continued violence and disincentives to settlement which arise during the course of the war itself. As Chapter 2 argues, uncovering the incentives for violent conflict not only reveals a more nuanced picture of the reasons for war from the perspective of the belligerents themselves, but also provides potential targets for outside mediators wishing to hasten the conclusion of a durable peace accord. External powers are unlikely to be able to influence the individual actions of combatants or the deeply held convictions or identities of the belligerent parties. But in all civil wars, trying to understand the structure of violence – why belligerents choose to battle on even when doing so would seem to be in their own worst interest – can help uncover avenues of influence for third parties whose interests are threatened by the continuation of armed conflict.

chapter 2

The Structure Of Civil Wars

While the dynamics behind each violent conflict are largely idiosyncratic, understanding the structural aspects of war-making in
internal conflicts can help explain the relative rarity of negotiated
settlements and the tendency of belligerents to continue fighting
even when doing so does not seem, on the surface, to be in their own
best interest. Beyond the apparent irrationality of violence or the
contested values at the root of many civil wars, there are other
factors which keep parties from the negotiating table and encourage
them to renege on commitments once peace accords have been
signed. Men may do the worst of things, Burke wrote, without being
the worst of men.[1] Uncovering the incentives for violence should be
the first step for third parties to take when considering their role as
potential mediators in internal disputes.

Structural Components of Civil War

As Clausewitz observed, war is not an act of senseless passion.
Belligerents often calculate the relative costs of continuing the
conflict versus reaching some kind of compromise settlement. These
calculations, however, are never as straightforward as they might
appear, for there are a variety of factors influencing the parties'
assessment of their own rational self-interest. In civil wars, at least
five factors can inhibit belligerents' ability to engage in negotiations
and strengthen the parties' interests in returning to the battlefield
after peace agreements have been signed.

Leadership

One factor that can frustrate negotiated settlements is the role of key leaders. Even if some members of both belligerent parties are willing to engage in negotiations and abide by the terms of negotiated settlements, the fears, attitudes and preferences of important leaders may be difficult to overcome. Particular leaders may be so committed to the struggle or to retaining power that they are incapable of contemplating some form of compromise with the enemy. For example, since the 1980s, the Sri Lankan government has launched a number of initiatives that would give the Tamil minority substantial territorial autonomy. Although these proposals have won the support of moderate Tamil leaders, the head of the LTTE, Vellupillai Prabhakaran, has remained opposed to anything short of a fully independent 'Tamil Eelam'. The intransigence of the LTTE leader, despite moderates' willingness to compromise, helped to ensure the continuation of the war throughout 1996. Similarly, as one author has noted about General Ratko Mladic, the former military leader of the Bosnian Serbs:

> [He] does not see Muslims or Croats as people fighting, however misguidedly, for self-determination, or for a multi-cultural society, or to avenge the injustices inflicted on them by General Mladic's own soldiers. They are for him the forces of Mordred representatives of foreign powers bent on the destruction of the Serbs.[2]

Such 'pathologies of leadership', in which élites effectively block any form of settlement because of their personal devotion to the cause, can prevent the signing of peace accords or even undermine their implementation after signing.[3]

Beyond their individual attitudes and preferences, the role of leaders can be problematic in another sense. As conflicts drag on, the distinction between the aims of the struggle and the personalities and perceptions of leaders charged with achieving them can begin to fade. Combatants on either side may come to identify their own leaders with the struggle itself, refusing to accept any negotiated settlement that would diminish the status of the wartime leadership. The equivocation between leader and cause can work in the opposite direction as well. A belligerent party may see the enemy leadership as the chief obstacle to settlement and may press for removal of the opposing élite as a precondition for negotiations or as an essential component of a peace accord. Moreover, in civil wars with a substantial international component, external powers may also conflate the personalities of leading élites with the stakes involved in the conflict, thereby encouraging belligerent leaders to identify themselves with the struggle. For example, US support for Savimbi in the 1970s and 1980s encouraged the UNITA leader to see his own survival as inextricably linked to the outcome of the Angolan civil war. Even though US involvement in

leaders may have a direct personal interest in continuing the war

Angola shifted from backing UNITA to brokering a peace accord, the previous support for his cause encouraged Savimbi to reject his defeat in the 1992 elections and return to the battlefield.

Leaders may also have a direct personal interest in continuing the war even when they know they will lose. How a war ends always affects the status of the political leaders who helped prosecute it. In both inter- and intra-state wars, leaders who are unable to produce a military victory are likely to suffer, either at the hands of the victors or at the hands of their own domestic constituencies dissatisfied with the ignominious outcome. Under these conditions, political leaders may calculate that betting on the slight chance of a military victory is preferable to accepting defeat and risking the wrath of the victorious power or of their own followers. A negotiated settlement, which might represent a moderate loss for political leaders, can be construed as less desirable than an outright victory, even if the immediate cost of attaining victory outweighs the cost of a negotiated settlement. Although accepting defeat or agreeing to negotiations might entail fewer costs than pressing for total victory, political leaders – thinking of the consequences of defeat for themselves – may decide to carry on the fight.

Such behaviour, which has been termed 'gambling for resurrection', is especially likely in wars that take place within states.[4] The stakes in civil wars are frequently seen as all-or-nothing: the state is either united or partitioned, the government is controlled by either one party or the other. Leaders on both sides thus have an incentive to gamble on the chance of attaining a military victory, even if the odds of winning are relatively low. Because they understand that a military defeat is likely to have serious consequences for themselves – at a minimum, removal from office, and at a maximum, exile or death – they have a strong incentive to continue fighting even if they feel that the odds of attaining victory are slim. The prospect of loss is frequently a more powerful motivator than the prospect of gain; when victory is uncertain, leaders may reason that pushing for an uncertain victory on the battlefield is preferable to the certainty of *de facto* defeat at the bargaining table.

In addition, leaders may perceive that fighting on, and even losing, would be preferable to returning to the situation which existed before the war. For example, the LTTE leadership – composed largely of non-Vellala-caste Tamils – has been motivated in part by its reluctance to return to a stage at which the Vellala held sway within intra-Tamil communal politics. The conflict in Sri Lanka thus concerns both dominance within the Tamil ethnic group as well as relations between Tamils and the Sinhalese majority. LTTE leaders understand that losing the struggle against Colombo could also mean losing their battles with rival Tamil castes, and gambling on the possibility of winning is preferable to negotiating and risking a resurgence of Vellala dominance.

Factional struggles within a belligerent elite, especially common in intra-state armed conflicts, exacerbate the leadership's desire to obtain a military victory even when the probability of success is low. Leaders understand that defeat, even the moderate defeat represented by a negotiated settlement, is likely to be used as a pretext for unseating them by rival factions within their own camp. Hoping to secure their personal positions against a dissatisfied public, erstwhile allies may blame the current leadership for failing to secure victory; internecine struggles for dominance within the belligerent elite may then supplant the struggle against the enemy. Confronted with these possible outcomes, leaders may feel that gambling on the possible (but improbable) chance of winning may be preferable to accepting anything less. Rather than shortening the conflict, the rational calculations of belligerent élites can therefore prolong it.

Problems of Decision-Making and Enforcement

Another factor influencing the calculations of belligerents concerns the decision-making process and command structures within the contesting elite groups. In all conflicts, belligerents may be divided among themselves over the utility of continued war, especially as the magnitude of costs relative to potential benefits begins to increase. Identifiable factions of 'doves' and 'hawks' emerge and begin to debate whether cutting losses and negotiating with the enemy would be preferable to pressing on to a (still uncertain) military victory. These internal disputes can consume considerable time and energy and, at the extreme, may even involve factional violence between those who would end the war and those who call for its continuation. Who actually speaks for the belligerent side, who represents the real interests at stake in the conflict and who is entitled to determine when enough is enough are all issues that create rifts within belligerent parties during violent conflict.

The conclusion and implementation of peace agreements in Myanmar, Liberia and the Philippines has been blocked by factional violence within the warring parties. In Myanmar, although the leader of the breakaway Mong Tai army formally surrendered in early 1996, his former allies have refused to abide by his decision to stop fighting, preferring instead to protect their lucrative heroin markets in eastern Myanmar. The inability to settle the dispute with the powerful drug merchants has also affected Yangon's ability to negotiate settlements with the country's 16 other insurgent movements. In Liberia, similar disputes among rival leaders – in this case over diamond mines – have frustrated attempts to implement a peace accord signed in August 1996. In the Philippines, the initiation of talks between the Moro National Liberation Front and the Philippine government prompted the creation of a breakaway group, the Moro Islamic Liberation Front, which continues to fight for a wholly independent Islamic state on Mindanao. Clearly, so long as no unified assessment of the relative costs and benefits of continued warfare exists, there is little hope for a quick end to the fighting.

In wars between states, the workings of national bureaucracies and organisational cultures can come into play. Even if policy-makers all agree that ending a war would be in their own interest, the inertia of war-making may affect the timing of the decision to halt the fighting. Behind the rhetoric of 'all for the country', bureaucratic interests lurk; in fact, war encourages bureaucrats to identify their own institutional interests with those of the nation. How and when a war ends can clearly have an impact on the power and positions of bureaucratic élites. Defending institutional prestige, securing budget allocations, sustaining morale and ensuring organisational autonomy can come to overshadow the interest in ending the war at minimum cost. As Leon Sigal has observed:

> Wars may end, but the work of government bureaus goes on. There are still programs to promote and roles to perform, budgets to parcel out, missions to conserve or expand, careers to advance . . . As wars draw to a close, officials do battle on two fronts at once: on one, to bring the enemy state to terms, and on the other, to end the war in a way that best serves their organizational interests.[5]

Where one sits in the hierarchy of institutions engaged in prosecuting the war can therefore determine where one stands on the issue of when and how to end it.

All these problems also exist for incumbent governments engaged in countering an anti-government rebellion. Factionalism, bureaucratic politics and organisational cultures can affect war endings as much in wars at home as in wars abroad. In civil wars, in fact, the obstacles to decision-making are likely to be even more serious than in inter-state conflicts. Factionalism among warring élites is often extremely intense, with belligerent parties breaking apart and reforming, coalitions appearing and dissolving and erstwhile allies becoming sworn enemies. Even if relations within each elite group are relatively stable, communications between élites and their subordinates often present a serious problem to leaders intent on ending the conflict. The actual communications network – radios,

war encourages bureaucrats to identify their own institutional interests with those of the nation

telephones and so on – is often in poor condition or non-existent, and even if such facilities are available, the non-traditional nature of combatants in civil wars can inhibit the leaders' ability to communicate their desire to end the fighting. Guerrilla fighters, child soldiers and soldier-bandits, all of whom may be crucial to the war-making capabilities of the contesting sides, may be reluctant to lay down their weapons and return to civilian life. The culture of violence spawned by the war may make former combatants unwilling to surrender their weapons, even as part of a coercive disarmament programme (as during UNOSOM II in 1993) or an externally funded 'buy-back' scheme (as during *Operation Just Cause* in Panama in 1989).[6] Interestingly, fighters on the ground in civil wars are therefore analogous to bureaucrats in the national-security institutions of the modern state: both have their own interests in the way a war ends, and identifying these private concerns with the aims of the belligerent side as a whole can create a major barrier to terminating the armed conflict.

Military Means and Political Objectives

Politicians and military planners sometimes assume that the shape of the post-war settlement in civil wars is a function of the military situation on the ground. According to this view, wars end when one or both sides are willing to accept the situation on the battlefield as a basis for peace. That stage might be reached when one side eliminates its opponent's will or ability to continue fighting, when one side gains its objectives or when both sides determine that the likely military and political costs of continuing the war exceed the potential benefits. However, the gulf between battlefield and negotiating table can be vast. There are several reasons for believing that what happens on the ground may be of little relevance to belligerents in their calculations of whether to continue fighting.[7]

In the first place, civil wars by their nature involve a relatively small space for compromise among the belligerent parties. In some cases, belligerents may go to war over the territorial configuration of the state, with one side pressing for autonomy or independence and another side fighting for continued central control over a separatist region. In other instances, the structure of government may be at stake, with both sides vying for control of the capital city and the right to determine which group retains the upper hand in the central administration. In either case, the belligerent parties have little common ground on which to build a stable peace; the total victory of one side necessarily represents the total defeat of the other, and a search by either side for compromise solutions can result in a charge of treason. In such situations, both sides have a strong incentive to escalate the conflict, to take advantage of military successes and to see anything short of total elimination of the enemy as a form of defeat. Establishing firm military control over rebel territory, annihilating the fighting capacity of the enemy forces, destroying the entire enemy population or preventing the rival group from ever assuming control of central government structures may become the overriding objective of the belligerent parties. Any end to the conflict that falls short of these goals is unlikely to assuage either side. The military component of war-fighting remains foremost in the minds of leaders in both camps.

civil wars by their nature involve a relatively small space for compromise

Second, the periodic and changeable nature of fighting wars makes the assessment of military costs and benefits, and the correlation of these with overall political objectives, extremely difficult. Fighting forces in civil wars are often poorly equipped and provisioned, and must rely on foraging and banditry to ensure that they are adequately supplied. In such circumstances fighting tends to be periodic, diffuse and in some cases seasonal, as rainfall, floods and other natural phenomena prevent soldiers from engaging in sustained combat. Towns, roads, energy facilities, pipelines and other strategic assets may be taken and secured by one side but later forfeited in the face of inadequate supplies or changes of season. Superior logistics is the hallmark of the modern, successful fighting force, but logistical sophistication is more often the exception than the rule in contemporary civil wars. In such situations, leaders tend to make decisions incrementally, weighing the short-term costs and benefits of a particular move in relation to the decisions that came before it; the highly fluid and uncertain environment in which the fighting occurs, however, makes calculating the costs of any one move in relation to the entire campaign impossible.[8] As a result, measuring real military success can become a difficult enterprise. Elites may therefore discount the actual battlefield situation when assessing the costs of continued violence. In Cambodia, for example, the periodic dry-season offensives by both the Khmer Rouge and the coalition Royal Cambodian government prevented either side from gaining a military victory, and forced the poorly equipped and factionalised Cambodian armed forces to adopt a strategy of containing and harassing – rather than defeating – Khmer Rouge guerrillas.[9] Encouraging defections, constraining the guerrillas' ability to secure new recruits and preventing them from gaining sanctuary in Thailand became the government's main aims. Assessing the 'success' of the counter-insurgency effort is thus extremely difficult.

Third, war creates special interests. In many civil wars, the over-arching political objectives that prompted the turn to violence can become lost amid the grievances and interests produced by the war's prosecution. Belligerents may pay lip service to their original political goals, but their actual objectives can be transformed by the experience of war-making. At the extreme, parties to the conflict may actually have an interest in continuing the conflict. Anti-government forces may make use of the economic potential of rebel-held areas in order to finance the war effort. Insurgents may use local resources to overcome the disparities in wealth and war-making potential between themselves and the central government, or between themselves and rival factions. Oil in Sudan, diamonds in Angola and Sierra Leone, timber in Cambodia, heroin in Myanmar and opium in Afghanistan have all become resources used by belligerent groups to sustain war. In turn, the continuation of violence ensures that the funds raised by such activities remain solidly in rebel hands. Despite their professions of ideological purity, members of *Sendero Luminoso* in Peru have effectively transformed themselves in recent years from an orthodox Maoist group to a well-organised coca-producing and processing firm. Their control of Peru's Upper Huallaga Valley has placed the region outside central government control and has ensured a continuous source of drug-related income. *Sendero*'s control of these resources has been such a profit-making business for the movement that even the capture of its leader, Abimael Guzmán, in September 1992 did not adversely affect the group's activities. In fact, the removal of Guzmán, a hardline Maoist, may even have allowed more 'pragmatic' leaders within the movement to focus their energies on criminal activities. Similarly, in Afghanistan the *Taleban*'s profession of loyalty to *shari'a* law has not prevented the group from extracting substantial profits from the country's heroin trade. Rather than prohibiting the cultivation of poppy plants, the *Taleban* have actually imposed a unified tax on opium production in the areas under their control, the revenues of which were used to fund the assault on Kabul in late 1996.[10]

War can clearly be profitable. But beyond the individuals who benefit from the exploitation of natural resources and the financing of rebel forces, non-combatant populations in rebel-controlled areas may derive substantial benefit from this 'occupation' by the insurgents. In states in which government structures are unevenly developed, anti-government groups may provide a rudimentary system of social services – providing some degree of security and social order and, in the process, ensuring the allegiance of local populations in regions in which official government structures are least visible. Between the withdrawal of the Indian peacekeeping force in 1990 and a new military offensive by the Sri Lankan government in 1995, Tamil separatists established an effective mini-state in Sri Lanka's northern Jaffna peninsula. Although the central government provided some support for the region's inhabitants, the police, courts and local economy were all controlled by the LTTE. Some insurgent groups, such as the *Fuerzas Armadas Revolucionarias de Colombia* (FARC), may be able to maintain an impressive array of social services in areas under their control, including such sophisticated economic transactions as the provision of low-interest loans to peasants and farmers. In Peru, *Sendero Luminoso*'s struggle against the government has actually helped create the movement's own social base. *Sendero*'s harassing of peasants and its control of agricultural areas in the Andean highlands have forced the migration of Quechua- and Aymará-

war can clearly

be profitable

speaking Indians to *pueblos jóvenes*. Offering no official social services and few prospects for work, these shanty towns have become major recruiting grounds for *Sendero* and for Peru's other major insurgent group, the *Movimiento Revolucionario Túpac Amaru* (MRTA) – in spite of the fact that *Sendero* was largely responsible for the dislocation of peasants to the shanty towns in the first place. The conflict has, strangely, become its own cause.

Furthermore, in instances of what non-governmental organisations (NGOs) call 'complex human emergencies', such as wars compounded by drought or other disasters, international aid can become one of the spoils of war. Conflicts in Sudan and Sierra Leone, among others, have been characterised by the efforts of rival factions to secure control over food and other forms of assistance – aid which was originally intended to alleviate the effects of the war on non-combatants.[11] Perversely, continuing the war can become an economically more attractive option for belligerents than ending it.

Neighbouring powers can also profit. States bordering war zones normally lament the economic costs and security threat of refugees flooding across their frontiers, and foreign governments and NGOs have often responded to calls for increased assistance to front-line states by delivering humanitarian aid and establishing refugee centres outside the conflict zone. The assumption is that neighbouring states are most interested in an end to the war and the quick repatriation of refugees, since dislocated populations inevitably represent a drain on the resources of the host country. For example, the exodus of over 1m Rwandans in 1994 sparked violence in eastern Zaire among Hutu and Tutsi refugees, as well as among the refugees and indigenous Zairean militias. In late 1996, a new round of fighting began, this time involving the Tutsi-dominated Rwandan army, Zairean troops, Hutu refugees, Hutu *interahamwe* militias and indigenous Zairean Tutsis. In some cases, however, refugees can actually be a boon for host governments; Zaire provides an instructive example of the potential benefits of conflict for neighbouring states. According to the United Nations High Commissioner for Refugees, local governors in eastern Zaire were loath to facilitate the repatriation of Hutu refugees to Rwanda. Local officials profited from the sale of petrol and supplies to the United Nations and NGOs working in the camps. Low-level conflict in the region ensured a continued international presence and a constant source of capital for provincial businessmen.[12]

Each of these scenarios illustrates why, in civil wars, there may be little correlation between the military situation on the ground and the willingness of belligerents (and their external supporters) to end the fighting, especially via negotiations. The nature of intra-state warfare encourages the contesting parties to see the conflict as a zero-sum game, prompting them to continue fighting with little regard for the costs. The periodic and often seasonal character of war-making can also mean that assessing military progress is extremely difficult, leading political leaders to press ahead for total victory without exploring other, compromise settlements. Finally, the economic incentives for continuing the war – especially in cases in which one side controls considerable economic resources and ensures the allegiance of local populations through their distribution, or in which international aid becomes one of the objects of war-fighting – also discourage belligerents from thinking about the relationship between military and political goals.

The Assymetry of Conflict

Another obstacle to the termination of intra-state wars is the often assymetrical relationship between the contesting parties.[13] Negotiated settlements to conflicts are most likely in situations in which opponents are roughly equal in terms of power, resources and goals. Such conflicts lend themselves to negotiated settlement for three reasons. First, when opponents share a common perception of the issues at stake, they are more likely to adopt similar strategies for settling the dispute. Reaching clear agreement on the root causes of the conflict is often the first step towards settlement, and if the disputants already share relatively similar views on why the conflict erupted in the first place, they are more likely to continue with negotiations. Second, symmetrical relations between the contesting parties encourage conciliatory behaviour, since each side possesses an effective veto over the pace and outcome of the negotiating process. Symmetry of power and resources can dissuade either side from attempting to undermine the position of the other and take advantage of weaknesses in the opponent's bargaining position. Third, symmetry of resources and goals means that both parties are likely to engage in similar calculations of the relative costs and benefits of continuing the conflict versus reaching some form of settlement. If the cost–benefit calculations of the contesting sides proceed in a reasonably similar fashion, then both sides will normally agree on the utility of moving towards a resolution to the dispute.

Rarely, however, do civil wars display this degree of symmetry among belligerents. Indeed, civil wars are almost always marked by great disparities among the various sides in the conflict in terms of their commitment, status and organisation. Each of these axes of asymmetry helps explain the intractability of civil wars and the inability of belligerents to reach stable negotiated settlements.

Commitment

Belligerents in civil wars normally display varying levels of commitment to their overall objectives. Particularly if the civil war involves a contest between an insurgent force and the well-formed army of an incumbent group, countering the insurgency is only one of a number of issues that the incumbents must address. As representatives of central state authority, the incumbents will be responsible for economic development, social services, foreign relations and a host of other concerns that have nothing to do with battling the insurgents. Especially if the insurgents pose no immediate threat to the stability and unity of the state, fighting the rebels may be relatively far down the incumbents' list of governmental priorities.[14] For the insurgents, on the other hand, seeking to overthrow the incumbent group is their chief *raison d'être*. Doing battle against central government forces – whether in order to take over the institutions of state or to change the territorial configuration of the polity – becomes the all-consuming goal of the insurgent group. The levels of commitment of an incumbent group and of an insurgent group, therefore, often stand in stark contrast. The former must balance its commitment to fighting the rebels with the many other tasks of everyday governance; the apportionment of resources to fight the insurgents is a constant pull on the dedication of incumbents. For the latter, however, the fight against the incumbent group tends to be all-consuming, since the very existence of the rebel group itself depends on its commitment, in short, to rebelling.[15]

This level of commitment can also change over time. At the early stages of a conflict, incumbents may simply ignore the demands of insurgents, especially if the latter pose no serious and immediate security threat. Silence on the part of the incumbents may breed further discontent among the insurgents, causing them to escalate their demands and resort to violence as a way of pressing their grievances. The outbreak of fighting can harden the position of the incumbent group, causing the leadership to strengthen its commitment to defeating the rebel forces rather than addressing their initial demands.

In addition, new political leaders on either side inevitably redefine the issues at stake in the conflict. They may downplay the goals of the previous leadership, shifting the emphasis away from the original intent of the former leaders and towards new objectives. In other instances, they may underscore the goals of their predecessors, seeking to reinforce their own position at the head of the belligerent group by portraying themselves as the rightful heirs to the aspirations of the previous leadership. In either case, the asymmetry between the commitment of the various contesting sides is likely to remain a salient feature of the conflict, since the level of obligation in each camp depends directly on the internal dynamics of each side, rather than on relations with the adversary. Internal disputes among rival leaders, debates between 'hawks' and 'doves' and evaluations of the success of military operations on the ground can all affect the degree of commitment within the belligerent parties.

Part of this problem relates to the issue of how belligerents analyse the relationship between their original war aims and the costs they have already incurred in their effort to achieve them. Practitioners of conflict resolution sometimes argue that getting potential negotiating partners to agree on the basic issues at stake in a dispute is of primary importance in resolving it; the role of the mediator is not only to provide a neutral forum in which the views of the contesting parties can be expressed, but also to help each side clarify its own view of the fundamental causes of the dispute and come to a more nuanced understanding of the perceptions of its opponent. In this view, conflicts can be reduced to a finite set of 'root causes', both real and imaginary, and identifying them is the starting point for the resolution process.

In civil wars, however, elucidating root causes can be problematic. The basic issue at stake in most internal conflicts is contested sovereignty: two or more groups vie for the right to decide the territorial configuration or governmental structure of the state. But in thinking about what actually drives the fighting and what impediments stand in the way of a negotiated settlement, the belligerents' own hortatory statements about the root causes of the dispute may be a red herring.

In the first place, in prolonged armed conflicts, belligerents analyse costs and benefits according to two rather different sets of criteria. The potential benefits of continuing to fight tend to be analysed prospectively, while the potential costs are normally viewed retrospectively.[16] Belligerents in civil wars can come to see warfare as an investment; the fighting may be prolonged in order to justify the costs, with little concern for any additional costs that might be incurred if it continues. In other words, recouping the losses already incurred in a conflict – atrocities committed by the adversary, the

hortatory statements about the root causes of the dispute may be a red herring

destruction of property, the damage done to international prestige, the death of revered political leaders and so on – can come to loom larger in the minds of belligerents than the further costs that might accrue if the fighting rages on. Justifying sunk costs, rather than avoiding future ones, can become the source of the belligerents' desire to continue the war. These calculations may then overshadow the putative root causes of the conflict itself and create yet another obstacle to a resolution of differences via negotiation.

Furthermore, root causes can become subordinate to the derivative grievances that arise during the course of a conflict. Historically, civil wars have been particularly fierce, often accompanied by genocide and other atrocities; by one calculation, around a quarter of all civil wars since 1945 have involved the attempt by one side to liquidate a non-combatant population associated with the adversary.[17] The way the war is waged can itself become a major point of contention between the belligerents, with either side refusing to negotiate because of actions taken during the course of the conflict. Waging a civil war can thus become a reflexive enterprise, with revenge for previous atrocities overshadowing the belligerents' pursuit of their original goals.

It should be stressed that it is not the *level of commitment* on either side, but rather the *asymmetry of commitment* between the rival groups that is at issue. The variable salience of goals on both sides prevents them from reaching agreement on the costs and benefits of continuing to fight. If the commitment of both sides were uniformly low, then presumably they would seek to end the fighting as quickly as possible and engage in negotiations aimed at settling the issues at stake. On the other hand, if the commitment of both sides were uniformly high, the salience of objectives might to some extent cancel each other out; the side that was able to muster superior resources would eventually emerge victorious, bringing a *de facto* end to the war by defeating the adversary outright or by forcing the opposing side to engage in negotiations. In either case, the conflict will move to a close more quickly than in instances in which the commitment of both sides remains relatively unequal.

waging a civil war can become a reflexive enterprise

Organisation
Another important axis of asymmetry involves the level of organisation among the contesting parties. Under conditions favourable to negotiations, the opposing sides are relatively well-formed, with strong and identifiable spokespeople, clear structures of command and lines of subordination, substantial solidarity among their constituents and clear boundaries of group membership marking the opposing sides. This allows the parties to negotiate effectively by reducing uncertainty and lessening the suspicions sometimes felt by both sides that their adversaries are negotiating in bad faith. It also reduces the chance that, once talks have begun, rival factions within either side will ignore the wishes of their leaders and seek to wreck the negotiating process.

In civil wars, though, the level of organisation among the belligerents normally varies considerably. On the incumbent side, the government is normally able to field a relatively well-organised and provisioned army, composed of professional soldiers or mercenaries, which can carry out multiple military operations over much of the state's territory. The government, moreover, is able to deploy its non-military resources – such as its foreign relations apparatus – in order to secure international support for the fight against the insurgents. On the insurgent side, however, forces are often poorly formed and composed of non-traditional combatants. Child soldiers, some as young as eight and armed with automatic weapons, have been important purveyors of destruction in Myanmar, El Salvador, Liberia, Peru, Sudan and other conflicts.[18] The lines of command are often indistinct, with combatants concerned more about survival than about long-term, strategic operations. The insurgents may receive material support from international sources, such as foreign governments or *émigré* and diaspora populations abroad, but they may lack the institutional structure to channel this support to fighters on the ground and to use it effectively against the incumbent regime. In Mozambique, for example, the *Resistência Nacional Moçambicana* (RENAMO) was unable to hold a united congress until 1989 because of internal factionalism, even though the movement had been battling the *Frente para a Libertação de Moçambique* (FRELIMO) government for over a decade.

In many cases, of course, the situation can be reversed. The incumbent forces may be poorly organised relative to the insurgents, with the former struggling to shore up its position against the fighting forces of the latter. In Sri Lanka, the LTTE has proved so effective against government forces precisely because of its secretive and diffuse organisational structure. Although the LTTE may have only around 10,000–12,000 fully armed and trained cadres scattered throughout northern and eastern Sri Lanka, the soldiers are organised into discrete, egalitarian 'cells', with members of each cell having little knowledge of the composition of other cells or even of their own rank within the military hierarchy. The soldiers are in turn supported by a wide network of 'catchers' who provide supplies and ammunition, and evacuate the wounded from war zones. This structure has allowed the LTTE not only to launch effective guerrilla operations and urban terrorist campaigns, but also successfully to engage government army and navy forces in pitched battles.[19] In Chechnya, Chechen forces held out for nearly two years against Russian Federation troops in part because of their highly diffuse war-fighting structure. While nominally subordinate to the late Chechen President Dzhokhar Dudayev and his successor Zelimkhan Yandarbiyev, Chechen field commanders were free to plan and launch their own direct assaults within and outside the war zone. Aslan Maskhadov, the Chechen Chief of Staff, was largely responsible for coordinating resistance against Russian troops in Grozny, while guerrilla *bandformy* (bandit formations) led by field commanders such as Shamil Basayev concentrated on discrete, high-profile operations like the hostage crisis in Budennovsk in June 1995. Not only were these two types of warfare largely uncoordinated, but they seem to have arisen largely as a by-product of factional disputes among Maskhadov and commanders in the field. The result, though, was to frustrate the Russian Army's attempts to consolidate its authority within the Chechen republic.

Although the structures of incumbent and insurgent forces often differ, the levels of organisation between the opposing sides are also normally quite different. Both have variable access to resources and differing abilities to employ those resources to wage war against the other. Such a situation clearly favours an outcome other than negotiated settlement. The overwhelming resources and superior organisational structures of one side can encourage escalation of the conflict, particularly when one side emerges victorious from a battle seen by that group as a turning-point in the struggle. Moreover, even if the more powerful side eventually seeks to turn from military might to negotiation as a way of ending the fighting, it may be unclear whom to approach on the weaker side with the offer of settlement. The party with inferior organisation may be divided into a variety of factions, each claiming to speak for the entire insurgent group. Designating the leadership of one faction as a legitimate bargaining partner is no guarantee that leaders of rival factions will abide by a settlement reached by negotiation.

Again, however, it is not necessarily the *absolute levels* of organisation on both sides that is at issue, but rather the *asymmetry* of organisation between the contesting parties. In situations in which the political and military structures of the belligerents are clear and well formed, legitimate spokespeople are available on both sides and there is little threat of intra-party rivalries coming to the fore, both parties are likely to be more amenable to negotiation as a method of settling the dispute. A negotiated outcome can also be a likely scenario in situations in which both sides share relatively low levels of organisation. If neither side can field an effective fighting force, garner international support, decide on a single legitimate spokesperson or engage in strategic planning aimed at winning the conflict through military means, moderate factions on both sides have an incentive to make contact with each other and to seek non-military solutions to their differences; they may, at the extreme, even become part of a coalition against their former allies who have refused to join them at the negotiating table. It is in situations in which the organisational strengths of the contesting parties are widely disparate, however, that some form of negotiation is least likely to take place. If one side retains the upper hand in terms of its ability to gather and deploy resources, it will have an incentive to decide the contest via military might. Even if the superior party decides to engage the enemy in negotiations, it will have difficulty identifying legitimate bargaining partners among the less well-organised group and ensuring that the rival leadership retains the allegiance of its fighting forces on the ground.

Status

Civil wars are characterised by serious disparities between the status of the various parties to the conflict. Status here refers to the way belligerents in the conflict perceive the identities and goals of their opponents, and to the way both sides in the dispute are perceived by external powers. Incumbents normally enjoy international recognition, a seat at the UN, membership in regional security regimes, some degree of popular legitimacy, foreign allies and trade relationships with foreign governments. Insurgents, while perhaps supported openly or clandestinely by external powers, have none of these. They are perceived by incumbents not only as threats to the security of the state, but as illegitimate adversaries as well. Their right even to participate in the conflict is often questioned by the incumbent group, which may characterise the insurgents as 'criminals' (as in Chechnya) or 'foreign agents' (as in Angola and Mozambique in the 1970s and 1980s) rather than as legitimate representatives of distinct interest groups within the polity. Incumbents may thus be wary of legitimating their opponents by recognising them as bargaining partners. It was not until its fifth Congress in 1989 that FRELIMO officially recognised the existence of RENAMO by calling the group by name.

Overcoming the asymmetry of status is often a major goal of insurgent groups and can represent an important step on the road to a negotiated settlement. Many civil wars involve a conflict over two separate sets of issues, one associated with status and the other with objectives. On one level, insurgents battle for the right of recognition, that is, for the incumbent party to accept them as a legitimate interest group with grievances that must be publicly addressed by the ruling elite. On another level, the conflict involves the actual substance of those grievances themselves, which are normally aimed at either changing the territorial configuration of the state or altering the constellation of power within the central government. It is at this first level of conflict that status asymmetries are most apparent and which in part accounts for the intractability of many internal conflicts. In some cases, in fact, the achievement of recognition by the insurgents – being accepted as legitimate bargaining partners by the incumbent group – can be a more important goal than the actual shape of the post-war settlement.[20]

The chief problem caused by status asymmetry is that overcoming it requires the incumbents to surrender their monopoly on defining the parameters of the conflict. In civil wars, incumbents always enjoy the dual role of umpire and participant: the incumbent party sets both the 'rules of the game' – determining who counts as a legitimate party to the conflict, how grievances are to be aired and what policy responses are to be made – while at the same time participating as an interested party in the dispute.[21] Insurgents, then, are always at a disadvantage. Not only must they contend with the incumbents' own objectives, their commitment to attaining them and the superior resources with which they pursue them, but they must also work towards their own goals within a framework of legitimacy and recognition created by the incumbents themselves. These two

incumbents always enjoy the dual role of umpire and participant

dimensions of conflict – over both status and substance – exist simultaneously in many civil wars and reinforce the difficulties that contesting parties often have in approaching the negotiating table.

Asymmetry and the Fungibility of Assets

Belligerents in civil wars instinctively understand the three axes of asymmetry outlined above. In fact, a major determinant of the evolution of internal conflicts is often the attempt by weaker powers to make relations with the adversary more symmetrical, or to tip the balance in their own favour. In this effort, the components outlined above – commitment, status and organisation – are to a certain extent fungible. That is, the weaker power in a conflict may trade some components of asymmetry for others, hoping that the greater weight accorded to some will redress the comparative weakness of the others. For example, the weaker power in civil wars, often the insurgent group, may compensate for its relative lack of resources and international recognition by substituting commitment to the cause for the superior resources and leverage of the state; this 'over-investment in ends' can make finding common ground on which to build a negotiated settlement all the more difficult.[22] The result is that the incumbent side employs its authority and resources to escalate the conflict and force a termination via military victory, while the insurgents strengthen their commitment to their overall war aims. The bargaining positions of both sides harden to a point that neither feels capable of compromise.

In a similar vein, commitment to the cause can be substituted for organisational capacity. Especially during protracted conflicts, the solidarity of the weaker power can often wane, with fault lines developing among various factions that threaten the ability of the group to carry on the fight. Some members of the group may defect, seeking to build bridges with the adversary and pressing for an end to the conflict, or may challenge the legitimacy of the group's existing leadership. In such circumstances, leaders have an incentive to strengthen their commitment to the cause as a surrogate for organisational robustness. It is no surprise that during times of crisis, at moments that leaders perceive as potential turning-points in the struggle, the rhetoric of do-or-die and all-for-the-cause comes to the fore. This, however, is not necessarily directed at the adversary, but rather at members of the group itself, whose waning dedication threatens the ability of the group to continue with the conflict. Leaders may harden their positions on the goals of the conflict not so much to extract concessions from the opposite side, but to ensure the solidarity of their own group and the loyalty of their brothers in arms. Strengthening individuals' devotion to ends can thus be a substitute for organisational vigour. The side effect, however, is often a narrowing of the space for compromise between the contesting sides and the prolongation of violence.

Other such substitutions are also common. Belligerents may attempt to exchange status for organisational capacity, hoping to focus international attention on the moral terpitude of their adversaries and the justice of their own cause. Similarly, if commitment is low, they may attempt to strengthen the group by essentially buying off potential supporters and promising patronage and other rewards once the battle is won. The point here, though, is that it is not simply the irrationality of individual combatants or the irreconcilable nature of their identities and values that makes internal conflicts so intractable. The asymmetrical structure of the conflict itself helps explains why so few civil wars have ended in durable negotiated settlements.

The Security Dilemma

Another obstacle to negotiation involves the 'security dilemmas' faced by belligerents in civil wars.[23] In conditions of widespread civil violence, there are no impartial institutions to enforce the commitment of warring sides to desist from fighting and enter into negotiations. Any negotiated settlement that does not involve territorial partition will presumably require the belligerents to demobilise or fuse their fighting forces into a single, unified national army. But because of the vicious and often protracted nature of intra-state war, there is little trust between the opposing sides; each may prefer to reserve some fighting forces as a credible deterrent should the opposing side scupper the negotiated settlement. Both sides may actually feel that ending the fighting would be in their own best interest, but with no overarching institutions to guarantee their security, they have no alternative but to retain some residual war-fighting capability. These reserve forces, however, present a security threat to the opposing side, which in turn justifies that side's unwillingness to disarm and accept a negotiated peace. While ending the fighting and laying the groundwork for post-conflict peace-building might in the long term enhance the security of all parties, in the short term the absence of credible security guarantees encourages both sides to stay away from the bargaining table. Because of the institutional anarchy of civil war, belligerents may be encouraged to hedge their bets and refuse to negotiate even when they agree that ending the fighting would be preferable to continuing.

there are no impartial institutions to enforce the commitment to desist from fighting

In Guatemala, for example, the Ministry of Defence's refusal to disarm civilian patrols along the border with Mexico has been a major threat to the ongoing peace process. Trained and armed by the Guatemalan military, the patrollers were responsible for carrying out massacres against former refugees who had returned to Mexico after an accord between the government and the URNG on the return of displaced persons in June 1994 had been signed. Denouncing the returnees as 'guerrilla collaborators', the civilian patrols refused to relinquish their weapons since they perceived the return of refugees as a victory for the URNG and a threat to their own hegemony in the border region. But the attacks on refugees, most notably the massacre of unarmed civilians in Xamán in October 1995, undermined the government's credibility and delayed the signing of a general cease-fire until December 1996.

In Guatemala, for example, the Ministry the Defence's refusal to disarm the civilian patrols along the border with Mexico has represented a major threat to the ongoing peace process. Trained and armed by the Guatemalan military, the patrollers were responsible for carrying out massacres against former refugees who had returned to Mexico after an accord between the government and the URNG on the return of displaced persons in June 1994 had been signed. Denouncing the returnees as 'guerilla collaborators', the civilian patrols were unwilling to relinquish their weapons, since they perceived the return of the refugees as a victory for the URNG and a threat to their own hegemony in the border region. But the attacks on refugees, most notably the massacre of unarmed civilians in Xamán in October 1995, undermined the government's credibility and delayed the signing of a general cease-fire until December 1996.[24]

Structural Obstacles and Intervention Strategies

The sections above identified five structural aspects of civil wars that help account for the difficulty of fashioning durable negotiated settlements. Quite apart from the irrational zeal of combatants or the deeply felt values and identities which may have sparked the conflict in the first place, the structure of violence itself may prevent the belligerents from settling their differences at the bargaining table.

• *Leaders* can prevent moderates within their camp from forging links with their counterparts on the opposing side. Even if leaders calculate that they are likely to lose the war, there may be residual incentives for continuing to fight.

• The *decision-making structures* and *enforcement mechanisms* among belligerents are often diffuse and uncertain.

• The willingness of a belligerent elite to negotiate may have little to do with the *military situation* on the ground.

• The *asymmetry* of commitment, organisation and status among belligerent parties is not conducive to negotiations.

• The *security dilemmas* of internal conflict are analogous to those in the international system. Without over-arching institutions to ensure credible commitment, trust between belligerent sides is a scarce commodity.

Despite these structural obstacles, some civil wars do end through negotiations. Although such instances have been rare since the Second World War, they have been significant. Since 1988, major internal conflicts such as those in Namibia, El Salvador, Nicaragua, South Africa, Mozambique and Guatemala have been effectively halted with the help of negotiations. Chapter 3 examines some of the conditions under which belligerents can begin to overcome the structural obstacles to negotiations and, in particular, the methods through which external powers might aid them in ending the violence.

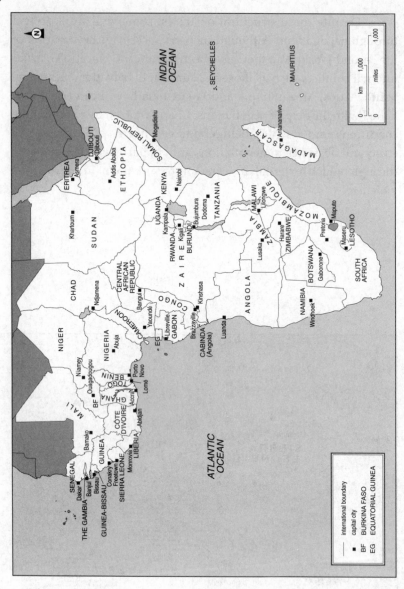

chapter 3

Strategies Of War Termination

As Chapter 1 illustrated, the diversity of outcomes to internal conflicts cautions against generalisation. Cease-fires have been important early steps in settling some conflicts, but not all. The promise of power-sharing arrangements has been a useful incentive for negotiations in some instances, but has been rejected in others. External powers have played positive roles in ending some civil wars, but the involvement of third parties – even as seemingly impartial mediators or providers of humanitarian relief – seems in other conflicts to have prolonged rather than diminished the violence. In addition, although analysts point to the ostensible lessons of past conflicts for current efforts at mediation and intervention, these 'lessons' often turn out to be arguments 'in support of doing – or more often, not doing – things that observers or policy-makers already have decided on'.[1]

There are, however, several conclusions that can be drawn from contemporary cases of sub-state violence. First, the end of the Cold War has had a variable impact on the tractability of internal conflicts; in some cases, the prospects for negotiated peace have been enhanced by the removal of the superpowers from the conflict equation, while in others the demise of East–West rivalry seems to have had little influence.

The end of superpower confrontation produced considerable optimism about the ability of external powers to promote peaceful, negotiated settlements to civil wars. Stripped of their importance as bellweathers of superpower competition, local conflicts were expected to diminish as belligerents' external patrons became less willing to spend financial and political capital on distant, interminable wars. Unlike the League of Nations, the UN Secretary-General argued in 1992, the international community had been given 'a second chance' to cooperate in the promotion of peace and stability, both within and between states.[2] Civil wars in Central America and sub-Saharan Africa, conflicts fed in part by the direct and indirect involvement of the US and the Soviet Union, were expected to move toward resolution; other potential conflicts, shorn of their significance to policy-makers in Washington and Moscow, were likewise predicted to remain dormant.

To some degree, the optimism of the early 1990s has been warranted. Far from being a period of global calm, the Cold War certainly had its share of vicious and protracted communal conflicts, religious struggles, urban terrorism and other forms of sub-state violence.[3] Indeed, warnings of a coming era of state dissolution and global anarchy notwithstanding, the actual number of hot wars – both inter-state and intra-state – has decreased considerably since 1989. Only in Europe and the Middle East has the number of large-scale armed conflicts increased, while the number of similar conflicts in Asia, Africa and the Americas has either remained relatively constant or dropped markedly.[4] In many of the archetypal 'proxy' conflicts of the late 1970s and 1980s – in Nicaragua, El Salvador and Mozambique – the end of external patronage and the active engagement of the United Nations and other international organisations have helped former belligerents to draft and begin to implement peace agreements. While many problems remain in each of these countries – such as reintegrating former combatants, clearing mines, rebuilding shattered economies and dealing with the legacy of atrocities committed during the fighting – the new environment of international cooperation has undoubtedly furthered the transition from war-making to peace-building.

In other countries, though, the post-Cold War world remains relatively unchanged. Belligerents in Sri Lanka, Sudan, Liberia, Sierra Leone and elsewhere have been little affected by changes in the global strategic environment. New conflicts have emerged, centred around differences of ethnicity, religion, clan, class and ideology. Even in conflicts fuelled by Cold War tensions – such as those in Afghanistan and Angola – the 1990s have brought little respite to populations for whom the difference between 'proxy' war and civil chaos has been minimal. In Afghanistan, the external dimensions of the conflict are no less significant today than in the past, with the raw national interests of Iran and Russia substituted for the US and Soviet rhetoric of 'freedom fighters' and 'international socialism'. In the West, both governments and publics have only now begun to realise what Angolans, Guatemalans and Sri Lankans, among others, have known all along: conflicts involving the well-organised armies of recognised states and prosecuted according to internationally mandated laws of war have been the exception rather than the rule in human history. All civil wars – whether during the Cold War or after – arise from an indistinguishable mix of religious, regional, ethnic, linguistic, economic or ideological differences. Just because the great global contest between rival social systems has come to an end, there is little reason to believe that the driving forces behind sub-state violence will become any less complex.

Second, the success of external powers in halting the fighting, rather than in assisting one side in the conflict, has likewise been mixed. Whether as individual states, regional organisations or international bodies, third parties have in many instances been unable to translate cooperation at the strategic level into conflict resolution on the ground. Interventions by Russian and CIS troops in Georgia, Moldova and Tajikistan, although successful in containing conflicts in these former Soviet republics and in reducing the overall level of violence, have not led to comprehensive settlements. Disputes between the Georgian government and the Abkhazians and Ossetians, the Moldovan government and the Transdniestrans, and the Tajik government and clan-based opposition groups in the

Gorno-Badakhshan region have continued with few signs of resolution. Similarly, multilateral coalitions have had only limited success in putting a definitive end to internal conflicts. In Liberia, it took six years for the forces of the Economic Community of West African States Monitoring Group (ECOMOG) to translate their presence into a negotiated settlement to the conflict; even after the signing of a peace accord in 1996, Nigeria's own interests in the outcome of the conflict continued to plague the agreement's implementation. NATO's first out-of-area operation, involving the deployment of some 55,000 troops as part of IFOR in Bosnia in late 1995, had a year later produced little optimism about the future of a peaceful, unified Bosnian state The same could be said for NATO's follow-on deployment, *Operation Joint Guard*, launched in December 1996.

Likewise, since 1989, the UN and regional security organisations have engaged in major peace-building operations in Namibia, Western Sahara, Mozambique, Somalia, Angola, Nicaragua, Cambodia and El Salvador, including efforts to sponsor peace talks, organise elections and demobilise combatants. Several involved attempts at brokering comprehensive peace settlements. Of these, all except Namibia, Nicaragua and El Salvador resulted in the defection of a signatory to the agreement and the resumption of violence. Even in the relatively successful cases, there were significant delays in the implementation schedule and continual threats by break-away factions among the belligerent parties. Similar efforts at peace-building in Bosnia could go either way. All these cases involved diverse forms of external involvement, ranging from mediation, through election monitoring and traditional peace-keeping to robust peace enforcement. With the possible exception of Namibia, none can claim to have been an unqualified success, for 'successful' negotiated settlements are always relative to the levels of violence and disorder that preceded them. In El Salvador, for example, the January 1992 peace accord led to the partial demobilisation of former *Frente Farabundo Martí para la Liberación Nacional* (FMLN) guerrillas and the country's first free elections since 1931. At the same time, though, there were serious irregularities in the voting lists prepared for the 1994 ballot; the elections returned a president with ties to former right-wing death squads and the newly created civilian National Police – the cornerstone of the peace settlement – was widely criticised for including members of the military who had engineered war-time atrocities.[5] In Nicaragua, the end of the war between the government and the Sandinistas did not ensure the pacification of the country as a whole. Former members of the army and the *Frente Sandinista de Liberación Nacional* (FSLN) guerrillas have become involved in criminal gangs in Managua, and in northern Nicaragua as many as 70 armed groups continue to battle government authorities.[6]

A third general conclusion to be drawn from the experience of external involvement in contemporary civil wars is that the protracted and persistent character of sub-state violence cannot be explained solely in terms of the irrational acts of individual combatants or the incompatible beliefs of the contesting sides. Indeed, seeking to address only the putative 'root causes' of the dispute can blind potential mediators to the economic, political and personal incentives for continued violence, some of which can emerge during the course of the war itself. These structural features of civil warfare – such as the disjuncture between military means and political objectives, the asymmetry between the various contesting parties and the dilemma occasioned by the lack of objective and credible security guarantees – all help to explain why some conflicts drag on even past the point at which it would seem in the best interest of the belligerents to stop the fighting.

the structure of conflict can prompt the collapse of agreed peace settlements

The structure of conflict can not only inhibit negotiations, but can also prompt the collapse of agreed peace settlements. In Liberia, the six main belligerent parties agreed to a cease-fire in August 1995 after six years of war, but shortly thereafter, the ULIMO-J faction led by Roosevelt Johnson defected from the cease-fire in a disagreement over the control of the diamond-rich areas of the country. In Colombia, successive rounds of negotiations with the country's numerous insurgent 'movements' and 'fronts' have led to the demobilisation of some factions and the signing of cease-fires with others. Yet the internecine struggles within each group and the ability of rebel commanders to profit from continued insurgency have made peace a distant goal. In Sri Lanka, an attack by LTTE rebels on two navy patrol boats in April 1995 ended a 14-week cease-fire; the government argued that the LTTE had demonstrated its undying commitment to violence with the attack, while the LTTE held that the government had merely been using the cease-fire to increase its military superiority over the Tamils. As these examples illustrate, the structure of intra-state conflict can both slow the conclusion of peace agreements and undermine the durability of peace settlements once they begin to move from inception to implementation.

Chapter 1 noted that relatively few modern civil wars have ended via negotiations and that those which have led on to renewed violence, often between the original parties to the conflict. Whether this trend is reversible in the long run remains uncertain. On the margins, however, external powers can influence the incentives for violence. The first step for potential mediators is to identify those areas where the greatest impact can be made. Some factors are more amenable to influence than others, and crafting an effective strategy of involvement entails targeting particular pressure points where the actions of third parties are likely to be the most effective. Of course, there is no single template that can be applied to all conflicts, and not all the structural features of warfare sketched in Chapter 2 are present in every civil war. Perhaps the most one can hope for is a general floor plan that might indicate some areas where external agents can help augment the structure of violence and promote good-faith negotiations. Recent practice suggests several ways in which third parties can transform the structure of conflict and promote durable negotiated settlements. In many instances it is only the active participation of third parties that can alter the cycle of violence and build trust among the warring sides.

Targeting the Structure of Conflict
The Leadership Conundrum

The issue of leadership can be one of the most frustrating aspects of civil wars for outside powers. Recalcitrant leaders can block the initiation or conclusion of negotiations, and can scupper agreements during the implementation phase. Even relatively cooperative leaders can indirectly undermine peace settlements if opposing sides come to blame their situation on the enemy leadership. Opponents may require the removal of adversarial leaders as either a precondition for negotiations or as a component of the final peace settlement. Few leaders, though, are willing to accept a deal which necessarily entails their removal from office, prosecution for war crimes or loss of the political (and economic) capital acquired during the war. Such was the experience with the Bicesse peace accords in Angola. Because of the highly personalised nature of the civil war, in which Savimbi became identified by all (including his

negotiated settlements tend to be associated with leadership change

own group) with the war against the central government, neither side was willing to accept any form of power-sharing agreement. However, the winner-take-all electoral system enshrined in the May 1991 agreement created great incentives for Savimbi to defect once he finished second in the September 1992 presidential race. Angola is illustrative of the paradox that often accompanies attempts at negotiated settlements: the very requirement that allowed the *Movimento Popular para a Libertação de Angola* (MPLA) government and UNITA to sign a peace deal in 1991 – the rejection of power-sharing – proved to be its undoing a year later.

In framing their response to this conundrum, external powers have several strategies at their disposal. Each may be more or less politically palatable, depending on the international and regional context in which the target conflict occurs, and each must be tailored to fit the specific conditions at hand. None, however, should be eliminated from the outset, for the complex dynamics of civil wars often require extreme flexibility on the part of intervening agents.

Timing and Leadership Change
One strategy is to take advantage of leadership changes among the belligerent sides and to use the uncertain period after the departure of a key leader to press ahead with negotiations. In fact, one of the

few things that may be said with some assurance about war endings in internal conflicts is that moves towards negotiated settlements tend to be associated with leadership change on one or both sides.[7] Such was the case in Mozambique, where a change of leadership within FRELIMO in 1986 brought to power the more conciliatory Joaquim Chissano, who renounced the strict Marxism of his predecessor, Samora Machel. Under Chissano's leadership, FRELIMO gave up its status as a Marxist vanguard party and moved towards the initiation of talks in Nairobi in August 1989. Likewise, the death of Chechen leader Dudayev in April 1996 paved the way for further talks between the Russian central government and his successors, Yandarbiyev and Maskhadov, on ending the war (even though the cease-fire broke down after the Russian presidential elections in June of that year).

Changes of leadership – as a result of death or internal rivalries – can create opportunity for negotiations, providing periods when the basic stakes in the conflict are reviewed and when new leaders begin to reassess the utility of continued conflict. As the Chechen case illustrates, however, changes in the top leadership of one side do not always indicate the willingness of belligerents to follow through on their commitments to negotiate. The removal of a key leader may, in fact, close the very window of opportunity that it originally opened. Indeed, the absence of Dudayev sparked a struggle for power among his successors, particularly Yandarbiyev and Maskhadov, with each pressing ahead with the conflict as a way of undercutting his rival's power. Both of these cases suggest, however, that using leadership change as a catalyst for negotiations is likely to be effective mainly in situations in which:

- the presence of a key leader is the most salient factor inhibiting negotiations;
- successors to the leader are united in their desire for peace; and
- the successor leadership is more interested in distancing itself from the policies of the previous leader than in staking a claim to the leader's legacy.

External agents must tailor their responses to take advantage of the significant, if fleeting, opportunities provided by changes within the belligerent leadership.

Isolating Recalcitrant Leaders

A second strategy involves the insistence on the removal of a key leader as a prerequisite for negotiations or as a component of the final peace settlement. Such has been the tack followed by the international community in dealing with the Republika Srpska (Bosnian Serb Republic) after the deployment of IFOR in December 1995. The presence of Bosnian Serb President Radovan Karadzic and his military commander Mladic was denounced as a major threat to the stability of the 1995 General Framework Agreement for Peace in Bosnia and Herzegovina. Both leaders were indicted for war crimes by the International Criminal Tribunal for the Former Yugoslavia in the Hague, and although IFOR commanders were unwilling to arrest the Bosnian Serb leaders, their removal from power was seen as a precondition for the successful implementation of the peace accords. A similar strategy has been employed in Sri Lanka. Along with promises of greater autonomy and development credits for Tamil-majority areas, the Colombo government under President Chandrika Kumaratunga has attempted to portray the LTTE as a hindrance to the economic prosperity of the northern and eastern provinces. Rather than ensuring the political and economic rights of the Tamils, the government has argued, the presence of Prabhakaran at the head of the LTTE is now a hindrance to the development of the Tamil regions.

However, this strategy is likely to be successful only in very limited circumstances; it may, in fact, inhibit the process of negotiations and implementation. By labelling the presence of key leaders an obstacle to the peace process, outside powers may strengthen the link between the struggle and the personalities of the leadership and belligerent parties themselves. Belligerents on one side may rally around their leaders in the face of external opposition, while those on the rival side may increase their insistence on removing the enemy leadership as an uncompromisable component of the peace settlement. Such has been the case in the conflict between the Moldovan central government and separatist forces in the eastern Transdniestr region. During the brief war in 1992, both the Moldovans and Western governments repeatedly condemned the Transdniestr leadership as mere holdovers from the Soviet period, thus reinforcing Transdniestr commitment to its own leadership.

Although the fighting stopped after the intervention of Russian Federation troops in summer 1992, a long-term settlement has been blocked in part by Transdniestr's insistence that its war-time leadership remain in power. At the same time, the Moldovan government has been adamant that no special provisions can be made for leaders whom they consider originally responsible for the outbreak of violence. External powers must be careful to avoid the twin dangers of strengthening the resolve of one leadership to remain in power while buttressing the commitment of the other to oust them.

Protecting Leaders' Interests

Outside powers may help secure the commitment of belligerent leaders by guaranteeing their safety during peace negotiations as well as during the implementation of a peace agreement. Providing 'leadership security' ensures that élites are able to take the politically risky step of negotiating without fearing for their own political survival.[8] While such a strategy may violate the concept of a 'just peace', one common feature of relatively successful negotiated settlements seems to be for outside powers to provide some sort of guarantees concerning the security and survival of key leaders during and after negotiations, normally through a formal power-sharing arrangement as part of the final peace agreement. The prospect of war crimes tribunals, the arrest of belligerent leaders and assigning blame for atrocities committed during the war all create great disincentives for leaders to enter negotiations and generate equally strong incentives for them to renege on commitments during the implementation of peace agreements. As Stedman has pointed out, it makes sense for external powers to assign blame in civil wars only when they are interested in defeating one side rather than sponsoring a compromise settlement, or when

> **credible guarantees of the physical survival of belligerent leaders must be provided**

they judge that negotiations with the present leadership are impossible.[9] In any case in which outside powers deem that ending the war is more important than defeating one side, and in which they feel that élites on both sides represent reasonable bargaining partners, credible guarantees of the physical (and perhaps political) survival of belligerent leaders must be provided.

Most often, such guarantees will entail acceding to some of the war aims espoused by the belligerents – awarding control of significant portions of Bosnia to the leaders of Republika Srpska, for example, or granting diamond concessions to UNITA in Angola. For all the talk of the inseparability of justice and peace by many conflict resolution theorists, the successful termination of civil wars may in fact depend on compromising the former in order to secure the latter. In many conflicts, populations have demonstrated a remarkable ability to move beyond previous wrongs and get on with the task of building peace. Even in Cambodia, where the Khmer Rouge's accession to power in 1975 led to the deaths of as many as 1.7m civilians, former enemies have shown an extraordinary willingness to cooperate. By the middle of 1996, the Cambodian government had begun serious negotiations with a break-away Khmer faction. External powers must avoid insisting on the removal of key leaders in circumstances in which such a policy contradicts the broader strategy of crafting a stable peace.

Clearly, none of these approaches is likely to have the same effectiveness in all conflicts. In developing a policy *vis-à-vis* belligerent leaders, however, the fundamental goal is to achieve a careful balance of certainty and uncertainty. Leaders must be given sufficient guarantees of their own post-conflict survival to encourage good-faith participation in negotiations and to discourage defection from agreed settlements. At the same time, though, the negotiating process and the final peace settlement must be detached from the personality of the leaders themselves. So long as the belligerents see the survival of their leaders as more important than peace, there will be little chance of a stable, negotiated settlement to the conflict.

The Problems of Decision-making and Enforcement
Even if belligerent élites are committed to peace, they may have difficulty convincing their subordinates of the desirability of

settlement. The non-traditional nature of combatants and poor communications can inhibit the ability of leaders to communicate their desires for peace to their colleagues. The culture of violence spawned by protracted conflicts can discourage fighters from giving up their weapons and integrating into post-war society. The private interests created by the war itself, such as the desire of individuals to retain the positions of power to which they have been elevated during wartime, can also make enforcing peace a difficult task.

Potential interveners must recognise these obstacles and plan to deal with them before they become actively involved in helping end the war. In some instances, they may in fact decide that the diffuse and strategically disorganised nature of violence makes any effective involvement impossible. Such was the case in Burundi, Liberia and Somalia, where large-scale violence, although sometimes highly organised at the tactical level, may have no clear sources at the strategic level. In such instances, any external support for negotiations is likely to be ineffective, since it is unclear whom external powers should designate as legitimate negotiating partners. Furthermore, even if effective bargaining partners can be found, there is no guarantee that all belligerents will abide by the terms of the agreement.

In some instances, however, the lack of well-organised and unified decision-making structures can encourage belligerents to negotiate. Fault lines within a warring side can create incentives for negotiations by undercutting the power of those leaders most committed to continuing the war. Divisions within the Khmer Rouge, between a smaller group led by Ieng Sary and a larger faction headed (perhaps) by Pol Pot, have been manipulated by the Phnom Penh government to end the Khmer Rouge's control of areas in northern and western Cambodia. By mid-1996, the more conciliatory Sary faction had begun to talk seriously with Phnom Penh about ending its military campaign and making peace with the central government, perhaps in exchange for being allowed to enter the political mainstream in time for parliamentary elections in 1998.

Making the Battlefield Count
A similar set of problems found in many contemporary conflicts is the periodic and unconventional nature of warfare within states,

the economic benefits of conflict and the security interests of regional powers; all can contribute to the disjuncture between the military situation on the ground and the belligerents' assessments of the utility of continued warfare. As Chapter 2 argued, the battlefield can come to matter less, since an accurate assessment of military progress is often difficult for belligerents to obtain. In addition, their own economic interests in continued conflict and the perspectives of regional powers, who may benefit from the war, can prolong the dispute even when it would seem rational to stop fighting.

What can external powers do to make the battlefield count and to convince belligerents of the desirability of negotiated settlement? The scope for external influence in this area is clearly limited. If the fluid and unconventional military environment prevents belligerents from calculating how well the war is progressing, if their willingness to settle becomes increasingly divorced from their performance on the ground, outside powers will have little success in convincing them to negotiate. At the margins, however, there are at least two ways in which external actors can help reduce the gulf between battlefield and negotiating table.

Creating 'Turning-points'
In the first place, external powers should be sensitive to actual changes in the military situation on the ground, and highlight these as major turning-points. Key battles, military offensives and natural disasters will only change the strategic assessments of belligerents if they themselves see such developments as crucial to their calculation of costs and benefits. External powers can help by stressing to the warring parties the futility of continued violence, especially in the face of natural disasters or decisive battles. Timing is crucial. Potential mediators must be prepared to act as the military situation develops and to underscore the fact that belligerents would profit more from negotiating now than by seeking an uncertain military victory in the future. Such seems to have been the case in former

Yugoslavia, where Croatia's *Operation Storm* against Krajina Serbs in summer 1995 helped convince Serbia and the Serb leadership in Bosnia that they were likely to receive a more favourable settlement at the bargaining table than on the battlefield. Throughout the wars of the Yugoslav succession, there were other offensives that caused the belligerent parties to reassess the prospects of victory and defeat. The key difference in mid-1995, however, was that external powers were prepared to capitalise on the changing military situation and to help convince the most determined belligerent élites that negotiations were an attractive alternative to continued violence.

Making War Unprofitable

In addition, external powers can assist in severing the link between belligerence and business, for the profit derived by some combatants from war-making is often one of the most serious impediments to negotiated peace. The international community can work together to ensure that the business of war becomes increasingly unprofitable, especially in instances in which war profiteering has a substantial international component. In such circumstances, accountants may make the most effective counter-insurgency forces. For the Colombian government, for example, a major strategy in dealing with leftist guerrillas has been to undercut their sources of financing, principally among the country's drug cartels. Insurgent groups such as the FARC and the *Ejército de Liberación Nacional* (ELN) in Colombia receive much of their sustenance from an elaborate system of 'taxes' on coca growers and drug traffickers operating in rebel-held regions, a source of revenue that in 1994 brought in an estimated \$269m for FARC alone.[10] By one estimate, in the period 1991–94, this informal tax system, along with revenues from ransoms paid to guerrilla kidnappers, may have totalled as much as \$1.8bn.[11] Freezing bank accounts and confiscating assets at home and abroad has become a major component of the government's attempt to bring the guerrillas to the negotiating table – and far more effective than direct military attacks. Exposing the grey area between war-fighting and criminality, though, is frequently an unpleasant revelation for policy-makers more accustomed to conflicts in which all parties are discrete and easily identifiable, and whose primary interest is in winning the war as quickly as possible. Lewis Tambs,

US Ambassador to Colombia in the 1980s, pointed out the link between drug trafficking and rebel groups as early as 1984, but because of US support for the country's ongoing peace process, Washington strongly rebuked its own Ambassador and denounced Tambs as an alarmist and potential saboteur of the peace talks.[12] It is far more likely, however, that the talks would have progressed more quickly had Washington cooperated with Bogotá in cutting the ties between the rebels and the cartels.

Reducing Asymmetry
Commitment

The asymmetry of commitment between incumbents and insurgents can inhibit negotiated settlements by preventing the warring sides from coming to some agreement on the costs and benefits of conflict. As with decision-making and enforcement, however, the asymmetry of commitment is most often affected by changes in the internal composition of both sides and the environment in which they interact. Changes in leadership and developments at the regional and international level can increase or decrease the dedication of both sides. The case of El Salvador is instructive. Despite the signing of a cease-fire agreement in neighbouring Nicaragua in March 1988, the war in El Salvador continued unabated. Several rounds of talks were held between the FMLN and the government of President Alfredo Cristiani throughout 1990 and 1991, but these led to no firm agreement on the FMLN's demobilisation or to a comprehensive political settlement. By late 1991, however, several events combined to give added impetus to a new round of negotiations. Elections in Nicaragua in February 1990 led to the defeat of the Sandinista government and the rise to power of the United Nicaraguan Opposition under Violeta Barrios de Chamorro. Although Soviet and Cuban assistance to the FMLN had dwindled during the late 1980s, the collapse of the Soviet Union in August 1991 and the progressive pauperisation of Fidel Castro's Cuba

focusing on the regional dimensions of peacemaking

robbed the FMLN of important moral support. These regional and international developments were important catalysts for the signing of the El Salvadoran cease-fire, which took effect in February 1992.

So long as great disparities exist between the commitment of insurgents and incumbents, there may be little that external powers can do to alter the strategic calculations of the belligerents. In such cases, potential mediators can be most effective by being sensitive to the timing of their involvement, taking advantage of regional and international developments that might alter the commitment of the warring sides. As in Central America, focusing on the regional dimensions of peacemaking – by portraying peace talks in one dispute as part of a broader effort to ensure regional security – can be one small way of affecting commitment asymmetry. But as long as insurgents and incumbents remain divided in their assessment of the utility of continued combat, external powers will have little success in encouraging a negotiated settlement.

Organisation

External powers are likely to have a greater impact on the asymmetry of organisation in internal conflicts. Indeed, as with disparities in the status of the warring sides (see below), external actors are often responsible for such asymmetries in the first place. By providing arms, bases, advisers and other forms of assistance, external powers often contribute to the asymmetrical organisation that characterises civil wars. Targeting these external sources of support is important to convince belligerents of the desirability of negotiations. In Central America, the Contadora process launched in January 1983 by Mexico, Panama, Colombia and Venezuela was aimed at reducing the influence of foreign states in the wars in Nicaragua, El Salvador and Guatemala. The proscription of foreign bases for insurgents, the reduction in arms flows from outside the war zones, the withdrawal of external advisers and the cessation of foreign aid and support were prominent features among the 21 principles enshrined in the Contadora agreement of September 1983. These principles were included in the subsequent Esquipulas II accord, mediated by Costa Rican President Oscar Arias and signed in August 1987. Based on the regional initiative of the stalled Contadora process, Esquipulas II later became the basis for comprehensive peace treaties in Nicaragua and El Salvador, and paved the way for a series of negotiations between the Guatemalan government and the URNG.

Getting neighbouring governments to agree to such regional pacification policies, however, is never simple. Some states may have an interest in fomenting chaos abroad as a way of undercutting rival regimes, while in other instances states may find that the domestic political costs of trying to halt a war outside their borders outweighs the potential benefits of peace. For example, co-ethnic populations in India's Tamil Nadu state have provided a life-line to the LTTE in Sri Lanka. Weapons, fuel, uniforms and other supplies have made their way across the Palk Strait to the LTTE's redoubts on the Jaffna peninsula. Colombo has repeatedly attempted to enlist the aid of the Indian government to stop the flow of supplies and to assist in the capture of the LTTE leadership. Some politicians in India have favoured such assistance, not least because the LTTE is widely suspected of having arranged the murder of the late Prime Minister Rajiv Gandhi. However, the political costs of such involvement remain high. Not only are Tamil Nadu political parties generally sympathetic to the Tamil cause, but the memory of the ill-fated Indian peacekeeping force in Sri Lanka from 1987 to 1990 has made central military planners reluctant to repeat the mistakes of the past. As the Indian case illustrates, securing a regional commitment to peace-building is one of the most complex aspects of external involvement in civil wars.

external agents can have a powerful impact on status issues

Status

So long as one side feels that it not only controls the substance of the talks themselves but also the recognition of particular groups as legitimate bargaining partners, all-party negotiations are unlikely. Such has been the case in Afghanistan and the Philippines, as well as in less-intensive conflicts such as Northern Ireland. As with organisational asymmetry, external agents can have a powerful impact on status issues. External powers can pressure incumbents to recognise insurgents as legitimate bargaining partners. In the case of El Salvador, the direct involvement of the US in December 1991 was crucial to the peace effort. When Cristiani wavered on reaching accommodation with the FMLN, then President George Bush dispatched six senior State Department officials to negotiate directly with the Salvadoran president. At that time, El Salvador was the sixth largest recipient of US aid, and the American envoys expressed to the Salvadoran leader that failure to reach agreement with the insurgents would have an impact on the aid relationship.[13]

The prospect of post-conflict elections can be another important way of augmenting status asymmetry. Holding out the idea of internationally monitored elections can sometimes provide the delicate balance between certainty and uncertainty that seems to characterise successful peace settlements. Insurgent forces are assured of recognition as legitimate players, a chance to defeat the incumbent government at the ballot box and the guarantee that, should their electoral campaign prove unsuccessful, defeat will not entail their removal from the political scene altogether. Incumbents, on the other hand, are assured of fair representation before the electorate, a low-cost opportunity to defeat the insurgents at the polls and the prospect of facing the insurgents at another election if the former rebels should manage to garner a preponderance of votes.

Elections are not, however, a panacea. In fact, they are likely to be useful instruments of war termination mainly in cases in which status asymmetry has been a major issue in the civil war itself. In other words, elections are most effective in situations in which the recognition of insurgents as legitimate players overshadows the other issues at the heart of the conflict. In El Salvador, the promise of elections organised by UN observer and peacekeeping missions was a crucial component in hastening the war's end. A major goal of the FMLN was to secure the recognition that its objectives – obtaining human rights guarantees, reforming the police and judicial systems, resolving the issues of land reform and economic development policy – were legitimate. Unlike conflicts in Angola or Afghanistan, supplanting the incumbent government or creating a separate state were not primary objectives of the Salvadoran insurgents. In such instances, internationally organised and monitored elections can be a powerful acknowledgement of the legitimacy of the insurgents' interests and demands. In situations in which the belligerent factions are fundamentally opposed to co-existence – either because one side is bent on the destruction of the other (as in Rwanda, Liberia and Afghanistan) or the creation of wholly separate political units (as in Bosnia and Sri Lanka) – elections are likely to be of little value.

Facing the Security Dilemma

Perhaps the most important avenue from which external powers can influence the willingness of belligerents to reach negotiated settlements concerns the issue of security. As analogues of anarchy in the international system, civil wars are characterised by an absence of objective and credible security guarantees for the belligerent sides. With no security assurance other than their own fighting forces, belligerents are unlikely to approach the bargaining table; moreover, even if they do manage to reach some sort of negotiated settlement, the implementation of the peace settlement is likely to be frustrated by the parties'

external powers can help alleviate the security dilemma

unwillingness to disarm and leave themselves open to new attacks from their erstwhile bargaining partners. It is for this reason that even the most well-planned and well-financed disarmament programmes have run into serious difficulties. The security dilemma in such situations is so acute that one study has described it as the single most powerful explanation for the success or failure of negotiated peace settlements.[14]

The Importance of Simultaneity

External powers can help alleviate the security dilemma in several ways. One concerns the issue of timing. Frequently, the incumbent side in a conflict refuses to negotiate before insurgents agree to lay down their weapons; in turn, the insurgents, fearing the government's bad faith, refuse to give up their weapons until they are assured that their interests will be recognised and accommodated in the final peace settlement. Such a scenario has been frequent both in full-scale civil wars such as Mozambique and Angola, as well as in less-intensive armed conflicts such as Northern Ireland and the State of Chiapas in Mexico. External actors, though, can help in this regard by insisting on some degree of synchronisation. The 1991 New York agreements ending the war in El Salvador called for the demobilisation and reintegration of FMLN combatants along with the reduction in size of the Salvadoran military and the creation of a new, united National Guard and National Police, all under the aegis of the United Nations Observer Mission in El Salvador (ONUSAL). The FMLN had been unwilling to compromise with the Salvadoran government for fear that any moves on their part towards reconciliation would be used by the powerful military as the occasion for a new offensive. By synchronising the demobilisation of the insurgents with major reforms in the Salvadoran army, the peace accords helped reduce the mutual distrust among insurgents and

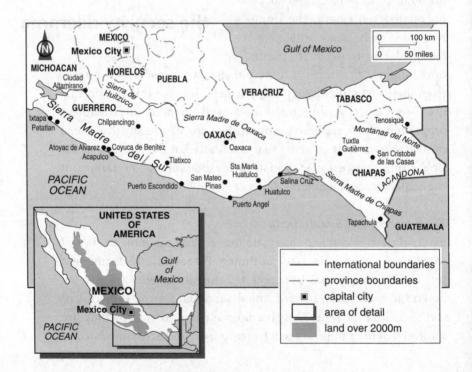

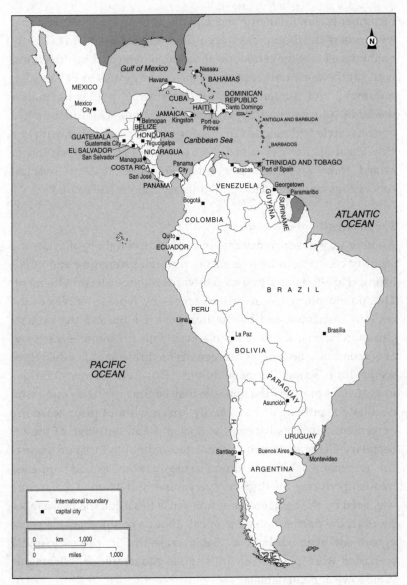

- international boundary
- ■ capital city

| 0 | km | 1,000 |
| 0 | miles | 1,000 |

incumbents. Simultaneity was equally important at the regional level, where the Esquipulas II accords attempted to provide security guarantees for all governments threatened by armed insurrections, while at the same time reassuring insurgent groups in El Salvador, Nicaragua and Guatemala that their principal political demands would be addressed in any future negotiations. Until that time, a 'vicious circle had plagued discussions about the conflict, with one side arguing that democracy had to come before suspension of armed force and the other side persuaded that no political concessions could be made until military actions had ceased'. [15]

The Ambiguity of Cease-fires

Another way in which external powers have sought to alleviate the security concerns of belligerents is through promoting and monitoring cease-fires as a first step towards a longer-term settlement. This policy, promoted at various stages by representatives of the OSCE in Chechnya and by the European Union and the Contact Group in Bosnia, seems to be in accord with a common-sense view of war endings. So long as belligerents are firing at each other, there seems little scope for negotiations. However, some situations indicate that precisely the opposite may be true: relatively successful negotiated settlements have easily arisen without prior cease-fire agreements. In El Salvador, the Special Representative of the UN Secretary-General, Alvaro de Soto, decided not to insist on a cease-fire agreement as a precondition to negotiations; as had happened frequently during the dispute, every minor infraction of a cease-fire was used by the belligerents as an excuse to scuttle the peace talks. By 1991, the parties agreed to speak about a comprehensive peace agreement even without a viable cease-fire in place.[16] Similar scenarios were played out in Angola, Mozambique, Nicaragua, Zimbabwe and Guatemala.

On their own, cease-fires can actually enhance the security dilemma rather than resolve it. Unless the parties are willing to engage in further negotiations, the cease-fire merely provides breathing space and time for belligerents to plan their next move on the battlefield. When these agreements are broken, the already scarce trust between the warring sides is further diminished. In fact, making a cease-fire a precondition for negotiations provides great incentive for extremists on both sides to escalate the conflict; so long as the fate of the negotiating process hinges on every shot fired and every grenade exploded, there will be little chance that the process will ever get off the ground. Moreover, even if a cease-fire holds, there is no guarantee that it will automatically translate into a stable, long-term peace settlement. In Georgia, cease-fires have been in place between Tbilisi and separatist governments in South Ossetia and Abkhazia since 1992 and 1993, but despite a series of negotiations sponsored by the UN and the OSCE, there has been little progress in forging a comprehensive settlement. In fact, the maintenance of an uneasy truce among the warring sides has decreased the sense of urgency felt by the parties and has led to the faltering of talks aimed at finding a long-term solution to both disputes.

External Powers and the Generation of Trust

Outside powers become engaged in internal conflicts for a variety of reasons, both laudable and pernicious. Even if the goals of involvement are commendable – reducing human suffering, promoting negotiations or protecting non-combatants – there is no guarantee that the engagement of foreign powers will ensure that these objectives are met. Indeed, UN operations in Somalia and Bosnia, the Allied coalition intervention in northern Iraq and the provision of humanitarian aid by NGOs to Rwandan refugees in Zaire suggest that in some situations external involvement can perversely assist those parties least willing to lay down their arms. In all three instances, external interveners were skilfully used by the warring sides, either as sources of sustenance or as shields against attack from their opponents, and inadvertently became a catalyst for rather than an inhibitor of conflict.

In other instances, however, third parties have been crucial to the success of negotiated settlements, often because of their unique role as an impartial yet powerful arbiter in situations in which belligerents have begun to question the utility of continued violence. In civil wars, external powers are often the only available generator of trust between the contesting parties. In the midst of protracted conflicts, characterised by atrocities, civilian casualties and wide-spread destruction, belief in the good faith of the opposing side is often scarce. By providing security guarantees to all belligerents during both the negotiation and implementation phases of peace settlements, international actors can play a major role in securing a durable settlement. External powers cannot themselves guarantee peace, but they can help alleviate the security concerns of the belligerents while they search for their own solution to the conflict.

Trust relies on the perceived legitimacy of opposing interests. In order to begin negotiations, belligerents need not see the demands of their opponents as legitimate; if they did, there would be no dispute in the first place. Rather, they must recognise the opposing sides as representatives of legitimate interest groups, even if they object to the claims put forward by those groups themselves. All sides must agree that their opponents are not merely terrorists, criminals or the agents of foreign powers. Once they concede that their adversaries' interests are more than chimerical, discussions can move to the substantive issues of crafting and implementing a peace settlement. Trust among the belligerent parties thus depends on each side feeling sufficiently secure in its own position to accept the legitimacy of contending interests and to discuss ways in which those interests might be accommodated in a final settlement.

external powers are often the only available generator of trust between the contesting parties

The ability of third parties to assist in the generation of trust is itself contingent on another kind of legitimacy, the perception that external powers have sufficient 'standing' in the conflict to allow them to intervene effectively without being perceived as favouring one side.[17] Potential mediators must remember, however, that legitimacy is determined locally. In civil wars, the weight of international law, the prestige of international institutions or the military might of individual states are rarely sufficient in themselves to provide third parties with the legitimacy and leverage to generate trust. The local acceptance of third-party assistance is, to a great degree, reflexive: the performance of mediators depends on their legitimacy, while their legitimacy waxes and wanes according to their ability to perform. There is no magic formula for resolving this dilemma, but targeting some of the structural aspects of civil warfare has in many instances been an effective strategy for generating trust among warring sides and for hastening the movement from war-fighting to peace-building.

Individual personalities and historical accident, misperceptions and vested interests all play such major roles in determining the outcome of civil wars that generalising about the paths by which they end is always a hazardous exercise. Even determining what counts as a civil war and how it differs from other forms of social violence can be a perplexing task, as can the attempt to identify at what stage an internal conflict has truly ended. Since the end of the Cold War, conflicts such as those in Zimbabwe, El Salvador, Nicaragua and Mozambique do seem to have come to a definitive end, with little chance of future violence between the former belligerent parties. But belligerents in other conflicts, such as those in Angola, Cambodia and Sri Lanka, have turned once again to violence even after signing comprehensive peace settlements and deploying peacekeeping missions. In still other internal conflicts, such as those in Somalia, Sudan, Peru, Colombia, Afghanistan and elsewhere, the end of superpower rivalry seems to have had little impact on the com-mitment or the war-fighting resources of belligerents. Contesting parties have made little progress towards negotiated settlements, and in some cases neighbouring states have stepped in to supply arms and other equipment once provided by the us and the Soviet Union.

The Cold War itself was framed by two civil wars. Both occurred in the same corner of Europe, and both, in different ways, set the stage for future debates about the role of foreign powers in internal conflicts. In the late 1940s, the war between the Greek government and communist rebels became the prototype for insurgencies in other parts of the world and strengthened the resolve of the US and its allies to combat communism in all its forms. In the 1990s, the wars of the Yugoslav succession have tested the ability of the international community to construct a stable post-Cold War security order and to quell what appears to be a rising tide of ethnic and religious discontent throughout the former communist lands. But whereas the Greek civil war set the US and its Western allies on a course of unilateral support for anti-communist governments in their drive for all-out victory, the Yugoslav wars were marked by multilateral, multi-track efforts to encourage compromise and the negotiated settlement of disputes. Promoting negotiations has supplanted victory as the chief objective of Western involvement in civil wars.

For all these changes, however, one thing has remained the same: the tendency of Western powers to gauge the relative success of their involvement in civil wars less in terms of the effect on the warring parties, and more in terms of the way that such involvement affects the strategic interests (and domestic politics) of those powers themselves. That external powers should be primarily concerned with the effects of civil wars on their own security interests is neither surprising nor censurable. Such a view does, however, complicate the creation of pragmatic policies aimed at hastening the end of internal conflicts which directly threaten the interests of third parties. While the international community stresses the need to halt the disintegration of states and stem the tide of communal violence, the effectiveness of outside powers in both regards is severely constrained by their inability to examine the incentives for violence from the perspective of the belligerents themselves.

Western powers gauge civil wars ... in terms of the way that involvement affects the strategic interests of those powers

The main contention of this paper has been that Western powers can begin to craft more effective strategies for involvement in civil wars by appreciating the structure of political, economic and personal incentives for violence. Rather than simply attributing the vicious and often protracted nature of civil wars to the incompatible identities, ancient hatreds or visceral animosities of the warring sides, Western governments must also recognise the rationality of violence in many civil wars and the structural obstacles to negotiated settlements. While irrational motives and irreconcilable values may account for some of the complexities of sub-state violence, other obstacles to durable settlements lie in the structure of warfare itself. At least five factors affect the rational decisions of the contesting sides and which explain why belligerents sometimes battle on even when it would seem in their best interest to stop. These include the role of key leaders and their personal interests in continuing the war; the problems of decision-making and enforcement on each side; the inability of belligerents to assess both military progress and the efficacy of continued combat; the asymmetry of commitment, organisation and status between the belligerent parties; and the security dilemmas inherent in intra-state conflict.

External powers can influence the importance of these structural obstacles, but their ability to do so is contingent on both the political will of the international actors as well as the nature of the obstacles themselves. Belligerents in civil wars are rarely able to overcome the structural obstacles to negotiations on their own. Expecting belligerents to do so, especially in prolonged conflicts in which each side has sought to take advantage of the weaknesses of its opponent, is to presuppose 'the existence of a "boy scout" spirit in circumstances hardly conducive to its development'.[1] There are several ways in which external powers – whether individual states, regional organisations or the international community – can assist belligerents in their effort to reach a negotiated settlement and to translate the agreement into a stable peace. While there is no single formula for all conflicts, external powers are likely to be more effective at reducing some obstacles than others. Influencing key leaders, reducing the asymmetry of organisation and status and providing credible security guarantees during the initial stages of negotiation and peace implementation have normally been the most important channels for external influence. Other obstacles, such as the asymmetry of commitment between the warring sides, have proven less amenable to influence from outside the conflict zone. Targeting those areas in which their affect is likely to be the greatest is the primary challenge for international actors.

appendix

Ongoing Civil Wars, Unresolved Internal Disputes and Areas of Major Internal Unrest, 1997

Country	Principal Participants	Onset of Violence	Major Current External Involvement
Afghanistan	*Taleban*, factions led by Burhannudin Rabbani and Abdul Rashid Dostum	1978	Allegations of Pakistani aid to *Taleban* UNSMA (good offices, 1994–)
Algeria[1]	G, FIS, GIA	1992	—
Angola	G, UNITA	1975	UNAVEM III (peacekeeping, 1995–)
Azerbaijan[2]	G, Republic of Nagorno-Karabakh	1988	Armenia (troops, 1991–) OSCE (mediation, 1992–) Russia (mediation, 1992–)
Bahrain[3]	G, BIFM	1994	—
Bangladesh	G, Shanti Bahini (Chittagong) guerrillas	1973	—
Bosnia[4]	G, Croat and Serb forces	1992	SFOR (peacekeeping, 1996–) UNMIBH (police training, 1995–) OSCE (human rights, 1994–)
Burundi	Hutu, Tutsi	1993	Allegations of Zairean involvement
Cambodia	G, remnants of Khmer Rouge	1975	—
Central African Republic[5]	G, Yokoma rebels	1996	Chad, Gabon, Burkina Faso, Mali, Senegal, Togo (mediation and peacekeeping, 1996–)
Colombia	G, FARC, ELN	1978	—

Country	Parties	Year	Intervention
Croatia[6]	G, Serbs	1991	UNTAES (peacekeeping, 1996–); UNMOP (peacekeeping, 1996–)
Cyprus[7]	G, Turkish and Turkish Cypriot forces	1964	UNFICYP (peacekeeping, 1964–); Turkey (troops, 1974–)
Federal Republic of Yugoslavia[8]	G, LAK	1996	—
Georgia[9]	G, Republic of Abkhazia, South Ossetia	1991	UNOMIG (1993–); Russia (military bases, 1991–); OSCE (mediation, 1992–)
Guatemala[10]	G, URNG	1968	MINUGUA (human rights, 1994–)
India	G, BSF, BLTF, PLAM, NSCN, Sikhs, Kashmiris and other factions	1981	Allegations of Pakistani assistance to Kashmiris
Indonesia	G, FRETILIN, Irian Jaya factions	1975	—
Iraq	G, KDP, PUK, INA, INC, SCIRI, other factions	1980	US and Allied Forces, *Operation Southern Watch* (no-fly zone, 1992–); US and Allied Forces, *Operation Provide Comfort* (security zone, 1991–)
Israel	G, PLO, *Hamas*, *Hizbollah*, other factions	1948	UNDOF (peacekeeping, 1974–); UNTSO (peacekeeping, 1948–); Allegations of support for various factions by Syria, Iran, other states

Country	Principal Participants	Onset of Violence	Major Current External Involvement
Lebanon[11]	G, *Hizbollah*, SLA	1976	UNIFIL (peacekeeping, 1978–)
			Israel (troops, 1978–)
			Syria (troops, 1976–)
			Iranian assistance to *Hizbollah*
Liberia	G, NPF, Krahn factions	1989	ECOMOG (peacekeeping, 1990–)
			UNOMIL (peacekeeping, 1993–)
Mexico[12]	G, EZLN, EPR	1994	—
Moldova[13]	G, Transdniestr Moldovan Republic	1992	Russia (troops, 1991–)
			Russia (peacekeeping, 1992–)
			OSCE (mediation, 1993–)
			Ukrainian and Russian Cossack forces (1992–)
Myanmar	G, KNU, NCGUB, other factions	1948	—
Nicaragua	G, FN380, remnants of Contras	1990	—
Pakistan	G, MQM	1995	—
Papua New Guinea[14]	G, BRA	1996	—
Peru	G, *Sendero Luminoso*, MRTA	1980	—
Philippines[15]	G, MNLF, MILF, NPA	1969	—
Russia[16]	G, Republic of Chechnya	1994	OSCE (mediation, 1995–)
Rwanda[17]	Hutu, Tutsi	1990	Allegations of Zairean involvement

Country	Parties	Date	Third-party involvement
Sierra Leone[18]	G, RUF	1989	Executive Outcomes (private security firm, 1995–97)
Somalia	Factions led by Hussein Aideed, Ali Mahdi Mohamed and others	1988	Ethiopia (troops, 1996–)
South Africa[19]	G, ANC, IFP	1996	—
Sri Lanka	G, LTTE	1983	Allegations of assistance to LTTE from India's Tamil Nadu state
Sudan	G, SPLA, NDA	1983	Allegations of Ethiopian, Eritrean and Ugandan involvement
Tajikistan[20]	G, IMT, other factions	1992	CIS (peacekeeping, 1992–); Russia (border guards, 1991–); UNMOT (good offices, 1994–); OSCE (mediation, 1994–)
Turkey	G, PKK	1984	Allegations of assistance to PKK from Kurds in Iraq
Uganda	G, LRA, other factions	1985	Allegations of Sudanese involvement
United Kingdom	G, IRA, CLMC	1969	'Mitchell Commission' and 'Twin-Track Process' (weapons decommissioning and mediation, 1995–)
Western Sahara[21]	G, POLISARIO	1973	MINURSO (peacekeeping, 1991–)
Zaire[22]	G, ADFLCZ, Mai-Mai warriors, other factions	1993	Allegations of involvement by Uganda, Rwanda, Burundi, Executive Outcomes and other groups

notes

Acknowledgements

The author would like to thank Michi Ebata, Jane Holl, Roy Licklider, John Nagl and Stephen Stedman for their helpful suggestions at various stages in this project. None of them bears any responsibility for the final product.

Introduction

1 See, for example, Ariel E. Levite, Bruce W. Jentleson and Larry Berman (eds), *Foreign Military Intervention: The Dynamics of Protracted Conflict* (New York: Columbia University Press, 1992); Arnold Kanter and Linton F. Brooks (eds), *U.S. Intervention Policy for the Post-Cold War World: New Challenges and Responses* (London: W. W. Norton, 1994); Richard N. Haass, *Intervention: The Use of American Military Force in the Post-Cold War World* (Washington DC: Carnegie Endowment, 1994).

Chapter 1

1 Roy Licklider, 'The Consequences of Negotiated Settlements in Civil Wars, 1945–1993', *American Political Science Review*, vol. 89, no. 3, 1995, pp. 681–90.
2 Bernard Gray, 'All the World's Serious Wars Were Civil Wars Last Year', *Financial Times*, 14 June 1996, p. 6.
3 John M. Goshko, 'Regional Conflicts Threaten 42 Million Around World, U.S. Study Finds', *Washington Post*, 5 April 1996, p. A16.
4 David Keen, 'When War Itself Is Privatised', *Times Literary Supplement*, 29 December 1995, pp. 13–14.
5 Christopher S. Wren, 'UN, Low on Funds and Successes, to Trim Peace Role', *International Herald Tribune*, 22 November 1995, p. 6.
6 Jeremy Harding, *Small Wars, Small Mercies: Journeys in Africa's Disputed Nations* (London: Penguin, 1994), p. 421.
7 John M. Collins, *America's Small*

Wars (New York: Brassey's, 1991), pp. 3–11.

[8] For a valiant attempt to bring some conceptual clarity to this issue, see Martin Edmonds, 'Civil War, Internal War, and Intrasocietal Conflict: A Taxonomy and Typology', in Robert Higham (ed.), *Civil Wars in the Twentieth Century* (Lexington, KY: University Press of Kentucky, 1972), pp. 11–26.

[9] Quincy Wright, 'How Hostilities Have Ended: Peace Treaties and Alternatives', *Annals of the American Academy of Political and Social Sciences*, no. 392, 1970, p. 61.

[10] I. William Zartman, 'Conclusions: The Last Mile', in Zartman (ed.), *Elusive Peace: Negotiating an End to Civil Wars* (Washington DC: Brookings Institution, 1995), p. 339.

[11] Stephen John Stedman, 'The End of the American Civil War', in Roy Licklider (ed.), *Stopping the Killing: How Civil Wars End* (New York: New York University Press, 1993), p. 182.

[12] Donald L. Horowitz, 'Making Moderation Pay: The Comparative Politics of Ethnic Conflict Management', in Joseph V. Montville (ed.), *Conflict and Peacemaking in Multiethnic Societies* (New York: Lexington Books, 1991), pp. 459–61.

[13] Fred Charles Iklé, *Every War Must End* (New York: Columbia University Press, 1971).

[14] James D. D. Smith, *Stopping Wars: Defining the Obstacles to Cease-Fire* (Boulder, CO: Westview, 1995), pp. 265–70; Michael I. Handel, 'War Termination – A Critical Survey', in Nissan Oren (ed.), *Termination of Wars: Processes, Procedures and Aftermaths* (Jerusalem: Magnes Press, 1982), p. 42; Janice Gross Stein, 'War Termination and Conflict Reduction, or How Wars Should End', *Jerusalem Journal of International Relations*, vol. 1, no. 1, 1975, p. 2; Gordon A. Craig and Alexander L. George, *Force and Statecraft* (Oxford: Oxford University Press, 1990), p. 229–46; Paul Kecskemeti, 'Political Rationality in Ending War', *Annals of the American Academy of Political and Social Science*, no. 392, 1970, p. 105; Morton H. Halperin, 'War Termination as a Problem in Civil–Military Relations', *Annals*, 1970, p. 87; Donald Wittman, 'How a War Ends: A Rational Model Approach', *Journal of Conflict Resolution*, vol. 23, no. 4, 1979, p. 744.

[15] For attempts to clarify the meaning and focus of conflict resolution, see Michael Banks and C. R. Mitchell, 'Conflict Theory, Peace Research and the Analysis of Communal Conflicts', *Millenium*, vol. 3, no. 3, 1974–75, pp. 252–67; John A. Vasquez, James Turner Johnson, Stanford Jaffe and Linda Stamato (eds), *Beyond Confrontation: Learning Conflict Resolution in the Post-Cold War Era* (Ann Arbor, MI: University of Michigan Press, 1995); John Burton and Frank Dukes (eds), *Conflict: Readings in Management and Resolution* (Basingstoke: Macmillan, 1990); John Burton, *Conflict: Resolution and Prevention* (Basingstoke: Macmillan, 1990); Dennis J. D. Sandole and Hugo van der Merwe (eds), *Conflict Resolution Theory and Practice: Integration and Application* (Manchester: Manchester University Press, 1993).

[16] Handel, 'War Termination', p. 44.

[17] Stephen John Stedman, 'Negotiations and Mediation in Internal Conflicts', in Michael E. Brown (ed.), *The International Dimensions of Internal Conflicts* (Cambridge, MA: MIT Press, 1996), pp. 354–55.

[18] Michael E. Brown, 'Introduction', in Michael E. Brown, (ed.), *The International Dimensions of Internal Conflict*, pp. 4–7.

[19] International Crisis Group, *The Dayton Peace Accords: A Six Month Review* (London: International Crisis Group, 1996), p. 23.

[20] 'Back to the Andes', *The Economist*, 22 June 1996, p. 45.

[21] Thomas A. Grant, 'The Protraction of Internal Wars,' *Small Wars and Insurgencies*, vol. 3, no. 3, 1992, pp. 241–56.

[22] Paul R. Pillar, *Negotiating Peace: War Termination as a Bargaining Process* (Princeton, NJ: Princeton University Press, 1983), p. 25.

[23] Licklider, 'The Consequences of Negotiated Settlements in Civil Wars, p. 684.

[24] Stephen John Stedman, *Peacemaking in Civil War: International Mediation in Zimbabwe, 1974–1980* (Boulder, CO: Lynne Rienner, 1991), p. 9.

[25] Chaim Kaufmann, 'Possible and Impossible Solutions to Ethnic Civil Wars', *International Security*, vol. 20, no. 4, 1996, p. 159.

[26] Licklider, 'The Consequences of Negotiated Settlements in Civil Wars, p. 686; Barbara F. Walter, 'Negotiating Civil Wars: Why Bargains Fail', unpublished manuscript, Columbia University, New York, 1996.

[27] See, for example, Robert Kaplan, *To the Ends of the Earth: A Journey at the Dawn of the 21st Century* (New York: Random House, 1996); Hans Magnus Enzensberger, *Civil Wars: From L.A. to Bosnia* (London: Granta, 1993); Martin van Creveld, *The Transformation of War* (New York: Free Press, 1991).

[28] William T. R. Fox, 'The Causes of Peace and Conditions of War', *Annals of the American Academy of Political and Social Science*, no. 392, 1970, p. 3.

[29] Carnegie Endowment for International Peace, *The Other Balkan Wars* (Washington DC: Carnegie Endowment, 1993), p. 11. See also Charles William Maynes, 'Relearning Intervention', *Foreign Policy*, Spring 1995, p. 110; and Enzensberger, *Civil Wars*, pp. 17–18.

[30] See Brian Hall, 'Rebecca West's War', *The New Yorker*, 15 April 1996, pp. 74–83.

[31] More sophisticated versions of this view have been explored by academic theorists of war termination such as Lewis Richardson, who focused on the power of 'war fever' in prompting and perpetuating large-scale organised violence and the task of finding a political 'vaccine' to ward off future armed struggles. See Lewis F. Richardson, *Arms and Insecurity* (New York: Atlantic Books, 1960), especially Chapter 22; and Anatol Rapaport, 'Lewis F. Richardson's Mathematical Theory of War', *Journal of Conflict Resolution*, vol. 1, no. 3, 1957, pp. 249–99.

[32] See Donald L. Horowitz, *Ethnic Groups in Conflict* (Berkeley, CA: University of California Press, 1985), pp. 564–76.

Chapter 2

[1] Quoted in Thomas Sowell, *The Vision of the Anointed* (New York: Basic Books, 1995), p. 3.

[2] Robert Block, 'The Madness of General Mladic', *New York Review of Books*, 5 October 1995, p. 8.

[3] Stephen John Stedman, 'Negotiation and Mediation in Internal Conflicts', in Michael E. Brown (ed.), *The International Dimensions of Internal Conflicts*, p. 485.

[4] See George W. Downs and David M. Rocke, 'Conflict, Agency and Gambling for Resurrection: The Principal-Agent Problem Goes to War', *American Journal of Political Science*, vol. 38, no. 2, 1994, pp. 362–80; Henk E. Goemans, 'War and Punishment: A Comparative Analysis of War Termination and the Fate of Political Leaders', unpublished paper, Harvard University, Cambridge, MA, 1996.

[5] Leon V. Sigal, *Fighting to a Finish: The Politics of War Termination in the United States and Japan, 1945* (Ithaca, NY: Cornell University Press, 1988), p. 23.

[6] See Mats R. Berdal, *Disarmament and Demobilisation after Civil Wars*, Adelphi Paper 303 (London: Oxford University Press for the IISS, 1996).

[7] This section arose out of a conversation with Jane E. Holl in February 1996. See also Holl, 'When War Doesn't Work: Understanding the Relationship Between the Battlefield and the Negotiating Table', in Licklider (ed.), *Stopping the Killing*, pp. 269–91, and *From the Streets of Washington to the Roofs of Saigon: Domestic Politics and the Termination of the Vietnam War*, PhD dissertation, Stanford University, Stanford, CA, 1989.

[8] Pillar, *Negotiating Peace*, p. 236.

[9] Trevor Findlay, 'Turning the Corner in Southeast Asia', in Brown (ed.), *The International Dimensions of Internal Conflict*, p. 198.

[10] 'Enter the Taliban', *The Economist*, 5 October 1996, p. 24.

[11] See David Keen, *The Benefits of Famine: A Political Economy of Famine Relief in Southwestern Sudan, 1983–89* (Princeton, NJ: Princeton University Press, 1994); and Keen, 'Organised Chaos: Not the New World We Ordered', *The World Today*, January 1996, pp. 14–17.

[12] David Rieff, 'The Humanitarian Trap', *World Policy Journal*, Winter 1995–96, pp. 9–10.

[13] This section draws from I. William Zartman, *Ripe for Resolution: Conflict and Intervention in Africa* (Oxford: Oxford University Press, 1985); and Christopher Mitchell, 'Asymmetry and Strategies of Regional Conflict Reduction', in I. William Zartman and Victor A. Kremenyuk (eds), *Cooperative Security: Reducing Third World Wars* (Syracuse, NY: Syracuse University Press, 1992), pp. 25–57.

[14] C. R. Mitchell, 'Classifying Conflicts: Asymmetry and Resolution', *Annals of the American Academy of Political and Social Sciences*, no. 518, November 1991, p. 32.

[15] I. William Zartman, 'Dynamics and Constraints in Negotiations in Internal Conflicts', in Zartman (ed.), *Elusive Peace*, p. 9.

[16] A slightly different version of this point is made in Holl, 'When War Doesn't Work; pp. 281–83.

[17] Licklider, 'The Consequences of Negotiated Settlements in Civil

Wars, p. 686.

[18] See 'Children in Combat', *Human Rights Watch Children's Rights Project*, vol. 8, no. 1, January 1996.

[19] Paul Harris, 'Tamil Tigers Intensify War to Establish Homeland', *Jane's International Defense Review*, vol. 29, no. 5, 1996.

[20] On the issue of recognition, see Charles Taylor, *Multiculturalism and the 'Politics of Recognition'* (Princeton, NJ: Princeton University Press, 1992).

[21] Zartman, 'Dynamics and Constraints in Negotiations in Internal Conflicts', p. 8.

[22] *Ibid.*, p. 9.

[23] See Walter, 'Negotiating Civil Wars; Barbara F. Walter, *The Resolution of Civil Wars: Why Negotiations Fail*, PhD dissertation, University of Chicago, IL, 1994; and Barry Posen, 'The Security Dilemma and Ethnic Conflict', in Michael E. Brown (ed.), *Ethnic Conflict and International Security* (Princeton, NJ: Princeton University Press, 1993), p. 103–24.

[24] See Human Rights Watch, *Guatemala: Return to Violence* (New York: Human Rights Watch/ Americas, 1996).

Chapter 3

[1] Chester A. Crocker and Fen Osler Hampson, 'Making Peace Settlements Work', *Foreign Policy*, Fall 1996, p. 56.

[2] Boutros Boutros-Ghali, *An Agenda for Peace* (New York: United Nations, 1995), pp. 39, 69.

[3] John Mueller, 'The Catastrophe Quota: Trouble after the Cold War', *Journal of Conflict Resolution*, vol. 38, no. 3, 1994, pp. 355–75; G. John Ikenberry, 'The Myth of Post-Cold War Chaos', *Foreign Affairs*, vol. 75, no. 3, 1996, pp. 79–91.

[4] Peter Wallensteen and Karin Axell, 'Conflict Resolution and the End of the Cold War, 1989–1993', *Journal of Peace Research*, vol. 31, no. 3, 1994, pp. 333–49; Peter Wallensteen and Margareta Sollenberg, 'After the Cold War: Emerging Patterns of Armed Conflict, 1989–94', *Journal of Peace Research*, vol. 32, no. 3, 1995, pp. 345–60; and Wallensteen and Sollenberg, 'The End of International War? Armed Conflict 1989–95', *Journal of Peace Research*, vol. 33, no. 3, 1996, pp. 353–70.

[5] See *The United Nations and El Salvador, 1990–1995* (New York: United Nations Department of Public Affairs, 1995); and Richard Stahler-Sholk, 'El Salvador's Negotiated Transition: From Low-Intensity Conflict to Low-Intensity Democracy,' *Journal of Inter-American Studies and World Affairs*, vol. 36, no. 4, Winter 1994, pp. 1–59.

[6] Hazel Smith, 'Any Sign of Hope for Nicaraguans?' *The World Today*, October 1996, p. 256.

[7] Stedman, *Peacemaking in Civil War*, pp. 240–41, note 19; Licklider, 'What Have We Learned and Where Do We Go From Here?' in Licklider, (ed.), *Stopping the Killing*, p. 306.

[8] Christopher R. Mitchell, 'Asymmetry and Strategies of Regional Conflict Reduction', in I. William Zartman and Victor A. Kremenyuk (eds), *Cooperative Security*, p. 45.

[9] Stephen John Stedman, 'UN Intervention in Civil Wars: Imperatives of Choice and Strategy', in Donald C. F. Daniel

and Bradd C. Hayes (eds), *Beyond Traditional Peacekeeping* (London: Macmillan, 1995), pp. 59–60.
[10] 'Drugs Provide Growing Revenues', *Latin American Regional Reports – Andean Group*, 7 September 1995, p. 6.
[11] 'Guerrilla Economics', *The Economist*, 13 January 1996, p. 40.
[12] Malcolm Deas, 'Narco Nabobs,' *London Review of Books*, 6 January 1994, p. 11.
[13] Marc W. Chernick, 'Peace-making and Violence in Latin America', in Brown (ed.), *The International Dimensions of Internal Conflicts*, p. 286.
[14] Walter, *The Resolution of Civil Wars*.
[15] G. Pope Atkins, *Latin America in the International Political System* (Boulder, CO: Westview, 1995), p. 323.
[16] Chernick, 'Peacemaking and Violence in Latin America', p. 286.
[17] I. William Zartman, 'Negotiations and Prenegotiations in Ethnic Conflict: The Beginning, the Middle and the Ends', in Joseph V. Montville (ed.), *Conflict and Peacemaking in Multiethnic Societies* (New York: Lexington Books, 1991), p. 531.

Conclusion

[1] Margarat J. Anstee, 'Angola: A Tragedy Not To Be Forgotten', *The World Today*, July 1996, p. 190.

Appendix

[1] Peace accord signed with UNITA in November 1994, but demobilisation of troops not completed by early 1997.
[2] Cease-fire signed between Azeri and Armenian forces in May 1994, but no comprehensive settlement.
[3] Around 30 people have been killed in sporadic clashes between the Sunni-led Bahrain government and the Shi'ite BIFM since December 1994.
[4] Peace accord signed between Bosnian, Croat and Serb factions in December 1995, but implementation problems still exist.
[5] A truce was signed in January 1997 between the government and army mutineers drawn mainly from the Yokoma ethnic group.
[6] There has been no major fighting between Croatian government and local Serb forces since *Operation Storm* in the Krajina region in August 1995, but United Nations troops remain in the disputed areas of Prevlaka and Eastern Slavonia.
[7] *De facto* cease-fire in effect between Cyprus National Guard and Turkish and Turkish Cypriot forces since August 1974.
[8] Serious violence began in Serbia's Kosovo region between local Serbs and Albanians in 1988, but 1996 saw an upsurge in violence attributed to the clandestine LAK.
[9] Cease-fire signed with Abkhaz region in July 1993, but no comprehensive settlement.
[10] Cease-fire and peace accord signed with URNG in December 1996.
[11] This entry refers only to the dispute over Israel's 15-mile wide 'security zone' in southern Lebanon. There are, of course, other unresolved issues concerning representation in Lebanon's central government and the disarmament of militia

groups in accordance with the October 1990 Ta'if Accord.

[12] There has been no serious fighting between the government and the mainly Mayan EZLN since December 1994, but several rounds of peace talks since April 1995 have produced no comprehensive settlement. The Marxist EPR first appeared in June 1996.

[13] Cease-fire signed with Transdniestr region in June 1992, but no comprehensive settlement as of early 1997. Russian troops remain stationed in Moldova both as peacekeepers and as remnants of the former Soviet 14th Army.

[14] In March 1996, the break-down of a cease-fire between the Papua New Guinea government and the BRA led to an upsurge in violence and a new government offensive.

[15] Peace accord signed with MNLF in September 1996, but violence continued with MILF on island of Mindanao.

[16] Cease-fire signed between Russian and Chechen forces in August 1996, but no comprehensive agreement on status of Chechnya within Russian Federation.

[17] Increase in violence in early 1997 attributed to Hutu 'death squads' attacking Tutsi survivors of the 1994 genocide.

[18] Peace accord with RUF signed in December 1996. Executive Outcomes formally announced an end to its mission in Sierra Leone in February 1997.

[19] A peace accord was signed between ANC and IFP supporters in the KwaZulu-Natal province in June 1996, but renewed violence has appeared.

[20] Cease-fire with IMT signed in December 1996.

[21] 'Settlement proposals' accepted by Moroccan government and POLISARIO in August 1988, and formal cease-fire in place since September 1991, but no comprehensive settlement.

[22] Spill-over violence from Rwanda began in 1993 and escalated to full-scale rebellion against government of Mobutu Sese Seko in late 1996.